BHAGWAT GEETA
Drops of Nectar

BHAGWAT GEETA

Drops of Nectar

R.K.N. BALI

KALPAZ

Bhagwat Geeta Drops of Nectar

ISBN: 978-81-7835-732-4

Published in 2009 in India by
Kalpaz Publications
C-30, Satyawati Nagar,
Delhi-110052
E-mail: kalpaz@hotmail.com
Phone : 9212729499

Laser Typesetting by: Quick Media, Delhi
Printed at : Young Art Press, Delhi - 92

CONTENTS

PREFACE

I had my early education at Rawalpindi, Mumbai and the higher education at New Delhi where we settled after coming from Mumbai. After Completing the studies I joined DCM (Sugar divison) where I worked for about six years and thereafter switched over to a Swiss Multinational Company (Nestle) where I worked till retirement.

After retirement the life has been very smooth and peaceful, but only the difficulty bing plenty of spare time at disposal therefore a thought came in mind to utilize the same in some productive and constructive work. Hence the writing of this book. Bhagwat Gita is a Vast Ocean of thoughts and emotions and I tried to take a few drops out of the same. How far I was successful, I leave this to the discreation of my esteem readers. For me personally it was a unique and spiritual journey throughout. It took me an year to complete this work.

I am grateful to my wife Rama, sons Amit, Ashish and daughter-in-law Ritu for their cooperation and support. I am thankful to my younger brother Brig V.K. Bali and Son Ashish who went through the manuscript and made the corrections where necessary. I am greatly indebted to my publishers for the assistance and support in bringing out this book. Without their cooperation it would not have been possible for me to reach my esteem readers. I have tried to keep the narration in a very simple language, so that this reaches to the wider section of Lord's devotees.

I dedicate this book to my late father Raizada Nand Lal Bali, who was a great devotee of Lord Krishna.

R.K.N. Bali

New Delhi

14–8–2008

CHAPTER I

Sanjay is Explaining About the Events Taking Place in The Battle Field at Kurukshetra to King Dhirtrashtra

धर्मक्षत्र कुरूक्षेत्रे समवेता युयुत्सवः ।
मामकाः पाण्डवाश्चैव किमकुर्वत संजय ।। (I-1) ।।

King Dhritrashtra asks his Minister Sanjay what do my and the sons of my brother Pandu's do, gathered for the war at the holy ground of Kurukshetra?

The forces of Kauravas (sons of king Dhritrashtra) and Pandavas (sons of king Pandu younger brother of King Dhritrashtra) were facing each other at the battle field of Kurukshetra. When the Pandavas brothers *i.e.*, Yudhistra, Bhim, Arjun, Nakul and Sahadev returned from exile and demanded back their kingdom from Kauravas brothers, they refused to hand over kingdom (Hastinapur) resulting in the war. This being the main cause. As the forces gathered in the battle field, king Dhritrashtra was in the capital city of Hastinapur. As he was blind, he asks his minister Sanjay to explain to him all about the war. Sage Ved-Vyasa bestowed powers of devine sight and hearing to Sanjay even through Hastinapur is four away from the battle ground of Kurukshetra, yet Dhritrashtra could get an accounting of events unfolding through Sanjay's devine sight and hearing capabilities.

So, Sanjay is explaining to the king about the situation at Kurukshetra, where the two opposing forces of Kauravas and Pandavas are standing against each other for the bloody war.

"दृष्ट्वा तु पाण्डवानी कं व्यूढं दुर्योधनस्तदा ।
आचार्यमुपसगम्य राजा वचनमब्रवीत्" ।। (I-2) ।।

Sanjay thus spoke to the king "After surveying the battle formations of the Pandavas army, your son Duryodhana goes to Guru Drona and speakes as under".

पश्यैतां पाण्डुपुत्राणामा आचार्य महतीं चमूम् ।
व्यूढा द्रुपदपुत्रेण तव शिष्येण धीमता ।। (I-3) ।।

Duryodhana asks Guru Drona to see the army of Pandavas and their formation and say 'This formation has been arranged by your own pupil Dhristhtadhyumna son of king Drupada". Guru Drona was the teacher of both Pandavas as well as Kaurvas, therefore it was but natural that his pupils were on both sides opposing each other in the battle field.

अत्र शूरा महेष्वासा भीमार्जुनसमा युधि ।
युयुधानो विराटश्च द्रुपदश्च महारथः ।। (I-4) ।।

"In this army of Pandavas there are great warriors like Bhim, Arjun, Virata and king Drupada."

धृष्टकेतुश्चेकितानः काशीराजश्च वीर्यवान् ।
पुरूजित्कुन्ति भोजश्च शैब्यश्च नरपुङ्गवः ।। (I-5) ।।

"Other warriors present *i.e.*, Dhrishtriketu, Chekitam, king of Kashi, Purujita, Kunliboja and Shaivya."

युधामन्युश्च विक्रान्त उत्तमौजाश्च वीर्यवान ।
सौभद्रो द्रौपदेयाश्च सर्व एवं महारथाः ।। (I-6) ।।

"Yodhamanyu, Uttamanga, sons of Subhadra (sister of Krishna), five sons of Draupadi. All of them are great fighters in their own fields. They are the main warriors in Pandavas side."

अस्माकं तु विशिष्टा ये तान्निबोध द्विजोत्तम ।
नायका मम सैन्यस्य सज्ञार्थं तान्ब्रवीमि ते ।। (I-7) ।।

Duryodhana is talking with Guru Drona and says to him "I will now tell you about our army and warriors too." He explains about the kings and princes who had come to fight in the favour of Kaurvas.

भवान्भीष्मश्च कर्णश्च कृपश्च समितिजय ।
अश्वात्थामा विकर्णश्च सौमदत्तिस्तथैव च ।। (I-8) ।।

"Besides your goodself (Guru Drona) there is our grand father Bhishma, and Karna (eldest son of Kunti and elder brother of Pandavas) our family Guru Kripacharya, Ashwatthama (son of Guru Drona) Vikarna and Bhurishrana (son of Somdatta)."

अन्ये च बहवः शूराः मदर्थे त्यक्तजीविताः
नानाशस्त्रप्रहरणाः सर्वे युद्ध विशारदाः ।। (I-9) ।।

"There are many other warriors as well, who have come here to fight in our favour and to sacrifice their lives for our cause."

अर्प्याप्त तदस्मांक बलं भीष्माभिरक्षितम् ।
पर्याप्तं त्विदमेतेषां बलं भीमाभिरक्षितम् ।। (I-10) ।।

"Our army is very strong because it is being led by none other than our grand father Bhishma. The army of Pandavas is being led by Bheema, but the same is no match against our army."

अयनेषु च सर्वेषु यथाभागमवस्थिता ।
भीष्मवाभिरक्षन्तु भवन्तः सर्व एवं हि ।। (I-11) ।।

"O Guru Drona I request you to take special care of our grand father Bhishma and cover him from all sides from the Pandavas army. So that they are not able to harm him in anyway."

तस्य संजनयनहर्ष कुरूवृध्दः पितामहः ।
सिंहनादं विनद्योच्चैः शखं दध्मौ प्रतापवान ।। (I-12) ।।

When this request was being made by Duryodhana to Guru Dronacharya, it was overheard by Pitamah Bhishma himself. He was very pleased and roared like a lion and blew his conchshell thus challenging the opposing forces *i.e.*, Pandavas army.

ततः शखांश्च भेर्यश्च पणवानकगोमुखाः ।
सहसैवाभ्यहन्यंन्त स शब्दस्तुमुलोऽभवत् ।। (I-13) ।।

There after all the warriors on both sides started blowing their respective conchshells indicating the start of the battle of Kurukshetra.

ततः शवेतैर्युक्ते महति स्यन्दने स्थितौ।
माधवः पाण्डवश्चैव दिव्यौ शंखौ प्रदध्मतुः ।। (I-14) ।।

Lord Krishna and Arjun sitting on a charriot driven by white horses heard this loud noise and they also started blowing their conchshells.

पान्चजन्य हृषीकेशो देवदत्त धनंजयः ।
पौण्ड दध्मौ महाशखं भीमकर्मा वकोदरः ।। (I-15) ।।

As Krishna and Arjun were blowing their shells the other warriors *i.e.*, Yudhistra, Bhim, Nakul and Sahdev also started blowing their respective conchshells thus indicating the start of the war.

अनन्तविजयं राजा कुन्तीपुत्रो युधिष्ठिर ।
नकुलः सहदेवश्च सुघोषमणिपुष्पकौ ।। (I-16) ।।

काश्यश्च परमेष्वास: शिखण्डी च महारथ: ।

धृष्टद्युम्नो विराटश्च सात्यकिश्चापराजित: ।। (I-17) ।।

When Pandavas warriors were blowing their conchshells the Kauravas warriors also started. Kashiraj, Shakandi, Dhrishta Dhyumna, Virata and Sataki blew their shells. This sends the warning that the war is going to start.

द्रुपदो द्रौपदेयाश्च सर्वश: पृथिवीपते ।

सौभद्रश्च महाबाहु शंखान्दध्मु: प्रथक् प्रथक् ।। (I-18) ।।

The five sons of Draupadi and the young son of Subhadra (Abhimanyu) were also present in the battle field. Each one of them blew his conchshell to register his presence. Subhadra was the younger sister of Krishna and married to Arjun.

स घोषो धार्त्तराष्टाणां हृदयानि व्यदारयत ।

नभश्च पृथिवीं चैव तुमुलो व्यनुनादयन् ।। (I-19) ।।

The warriors in the Kaurvas camp were frightened with the flurry made by the conchshells blown by the Pandavas army. The noise was so loud that it appeared earth is shattening.

अथ व्यवस्थितान्दृष्ट्वा: धार्तराष्ट्रान्-कपिध्वज: ।

प्रवृत्ते शस्त्रसम्पाते धनुरूद्यम्य पाण्डव: ।। (I-20) ।।

Arjun picks up his bow and surveys the battle field. He glances at the warriors gathered for the battle. They were all known to him, because all of them were his kith and kins.

हृषीकेश तदा वाक्यमिदमाह महीपते ।

सेनयोंरूभयोर्मध्ये रथं स्थापय मेऽच्युत ।। (I-21) ।।

Arjun thus speaks to Krishna "O Lord take my chariot in between the two opposing forces so that I may clearly see with whom I have to fight in this battle." Krishna takes the chariot in between the two forces as desired by Arjun.

Arjun see's so many relatives and friends ready to kill one another in the battle.

यावदेतान्निरीक्षेऽहं योध्दुकामानवस्थितान ।

कैर्मया सह योध्दव्यमस्मिन रणसमुद्यमे ।। (I-22) ।।

Arjun tells Krishna "O Lord I want to see with whom I have to fight in this battle and those people also with whom I should not fight." At this time a feeling of remorse comes in the mind of Arjun, before the battle, he is restless and confused.

योत्स्यमानानवेक्षेऽहं य एतेऽत्र समागता:
धार्तराष्ट्रस्य दुर्बुध्देर्युध्दे प्रियचिकीर्षव: ।। (I-23) ।।

Arjun says to Krishna "O Keshav I want to see those people who have joined hands with evil minded Duryodhana to fight against us."

एवमुक्तो हृषीकेशो: गुडाकेशन भारत ।
सेनयोरूभयोर्मध्ये स्थापयित्वा रथोत्तमम ।। (I-24) ।।

At this point Sanjay tells king Dhritrashtra that Krishna takes the chariot in between the two opposing forces as per Arjun's wish so that he could satisfy himself before the war.

भीष्मद्रोणप्रमुखत: सर्वेषां च महीक्षिताम् ।
उवाच पार्थ पश्यैतान्समवेतान्कुरूनिति ।। (I-25) ।।

Krishna takes the chariot and parks it in front of Pitamah Bhishma, Dronacharya and the other warriors. Krishna says to Arjun "O Parth you can now see your relatives and friends who have come to fight against you."

तत्रापश्यत्स्थितान्पार्थ: पितृनथ पितामहान् ।
आचार्यान्मातुलान्भ्रातृ पुत्रान्पौत्रान्स रवीस्तथा ।। (I-26) ।।

Arjun looks at the Kaurav's army. He finds his uncles, cousins, sons, gurus, grandfathers, friends and other near and dear relatives who all have joined hands to oppose him and his brothers.

श्वशुरान् सुहृदश्चैव सेनयोरूभयोरपि ।
तान्समीक्ष्य स कौन्तेय: सर्वान् बन्धूनवस्थितान् ।। (I-27) ।।

He sees fathers-in-law and many other relations on both sides; because all were related to one another and belonged to the same clan or family.

कृपया परयाविष्टो विषीदन्निदमब्रवीत् ।

Arjun becomes overwhelmed with grief and thus speaks to Krishna.

द्रृष्टवेमं स्वंजन कृष्ण युयुत्सुं समुपस्थितम् ।। (I-28) ।।

By seeing his own kith and kins in the battle field Arjun is sad and says to Krishna.

सीदन्ति मम गात्राणि मुखं च परिशुष्यति ।
वेपथुश्च शरीरे मे रोमहर्षश्च जायते ।। (I-29) ।।

"O Lord by seeing all my relations and friends I am very unhappy. I am getting extremely nervous and sad. My mouth is drying up and my body is shaking with grief and sorrow.

गाण्डीवं संत्रसते हस्तात्त्वक्चैव परिदह्यता ।

न च शक्नोम्य वस्थातुं भ्रमतीव च मे मनः ।। (I-30) ।।

"I am unable to keep my bow Gandeeva in my hand and it is slipping and I am unable to stand on my legs."

On seeing his friends and relatives Arjun becomes extremely sad and full of sorrow as he does not want to fight with his own people.

निमित्तानि च पश्यामि विपरीतानि केशव ।

न च श्रेयोऽनु पश्यामि हत्वा स्वजन माहवे ।। (I-31) ।।

"O Krishna, I do not want to kill these people as they are all my own relations. The signs are not good as the fate has brought us in this battle field." In other words Arjun is very remorseful and does not want to fight.

न कांक्षे विजयं कृष्ण न च राज्यं सुखानि च ।

किं नो राज्येन गोविन्द किं भोगैर्जीवितेन वा ।। (I-32) ।।

O Krishna says Arjun "What is the use of that kingdom where we have to do so much of killings. I do not want that kingdom, which we will get after killing our own kith and kins."

येषामर्थे कांक्षितं नो राज्यं भोगाः सुखानि च ।

त इमेऽवस्थिता युध्दे प्राणंस्त्यक्त्वा धनानि च ।। (I-33) ।।

"O Krishna, the people from whom we have to take back our kingdom, they themselves are standing here ready to sacrifice their lives and luxuries."

आचार्याः पितरः पुत्रास्तथैव च पितामहाः ।

मातुलाः श्वशुराः पौत्राः श्यालाः सम्बन्धिनस्तथा ।। (I-34) ।।

"What is the use of this kingdom which we get after killing our friends and relatives. I will not accept the same if I have to kill my teachers, sons, grand father Bhishma, father-in-law, grand sons and other relatives. So the kingdom of this earth does not have any meaning for me."

एतान्न हन्तुमिच्छामि ध्नतोऽपि मधुसूदन ।

अपि त्रैलोक्यराज्यस्य हेतोः किं नु महीकृते ।। (I-35) ।।

"O Krishna I feel very sad I do not want to kill my own relatives. Leave aside the kingdom of this earth, I will not accept the kingdom of this whole universe if I have to attain the same after killing my own people. I will not fight at any cost and I do not want such a kingdom."

निहत्य धार्तराष्ट्रान्नः नः का प्रीतिः स्याज्जनार्दन ।

पापमेवाश्रंयेदस्मान् हत्वैतानाततायिनः ।। (I-36) ।।

Arjun says "O Madhusudan how shall we get happiness by killing the sons of Dhritashtra? It will he very sinful and lead us to sorrow and unhappiness after this sinful act. Therefore, I will not kill them at any cost. Only curse will fall on us by doing so."

तस्मान्नार्हा वयं हन्तुं धार्तराष्ट्रान्स्वबान्धवान् ।

स्वजनं हि कंथ हत्वा सुखिनः स्याम माधव ।। (I-37) ।।

Arjun continues "O Madhav how can we live happily after killing them? We will be leading only sinful life after this mass slaughter of our own people." Arjun is in two minds whether to kill or not, he is confused and unable to decide whether to fight or not. At this point his mind starts vacillating.

यद्यप्येते न पश्यन्ति लोभोंपहतचेतसः ।

कुलक्षयकृतं दोषं मित्रद्रोहे च पातकम् ।। (I-38) ।।

कथं न ज्ञेयमस्माभिः पापादस्मान्निवर्तितुम् ।

कुलक्षयकृतं दोषं प्रपश्यदिर्जनार्दन ।। (I-39) ।।

O Krishna says Arjun "Although due to greed and pride, these people are bent to fight with us but why should we be ignorant to accept this. It will he very sinful, the coming generations will not forgive us for destroying our own people."

कुलक्षये प्रणश्यन्ति कुलधर्माः सनातनाः ।

धर्मे नष्टे कुलं कृत्सनम धर्मोऽभिभवत्युत ।। (I-40) ।।

"Due to this war there will be destruction of our Sanathan Dharma as thousands of warriors will perish in this bloody war. Our families and the entire clan will come to an end, as majority of the male members will die. So there is no use of fighting."

अर्धमाभिभवात्कृष्ण प्रदुष्यन्ति कुलस्त्रियः ।

स्त्रीषु दुष्टासु वार्ष्णय जायते वर्णसंकरः ।। (I-41) ।।

"With the killing of the majority of the males, our women will become sinful and produce impure breed which is equal to destruction of our pure clan. So it is improper to start this war. It will only bring sin and destruction to our society at large."

संकरो नरकायैव कुलघ्नानां कुलस्य च ।

पतन्ति पितरो ह्येषां लुप्तपिण्डोदकक्रियाः ।। (I-42) ।।

"Even our ancestors will not get mokshya because any ceremony performed by sinful people will not be pure at all. So our breed will become impure and fall into hell."

दोषैरेतैः कुलघ्नानां वर्णसंकरकारकैः ।

उत्साद्यन्ते जातिधर्माः कुलधर्माश्च शाश्वताः ।। (I-43) ।।

"Due to this impure breed our Dharma will also get destroyed. It will be the cause of our downfall."

उत्सन्नकुलधर्माणां मनुष्यांणा जनार्दन ।

नरके नियतं वासो भवतीत्यनुशुश्रुम ।। (I-44) ।।

Arjun says "O Janardana the society which has lost dharma rots in the hell. This is what I understand in this situation. Therefore I feel that this war is going to harm us."

These were the misgivings of Arjun, that is why he wants to avoid this war.

अहो बत महत्पांप कर्तुं व्यवसिता वयम् ।

यद्रांज्यसुखलोभेन हन्तुं स्वजनमुद्यताः ।। (I-45) ।।

"Arjun says to Krishna "We are intelligent enough but even then we are going to commit the crime of killing and destroying each other for the sake of luxuries and kingdoms. I feel that we should not do the same."

यदि मामप्रतीकारमशस्त्रं शस्त्रपाणयः ।

धार्तराष्ट्रा रणे हन्युस्तन्मे क्षेमतरं भवेत् ।। (I-46) ।।

"I will feel happy if the sons of my uncle Dhritrashtra kill us in this battle. But I will not like to kill them at all. Let them kill us, but I will not fight with my own relatives."

एवमुक्त्वार्जुनः संख्ये रथोपस्थ उपाविशत् ।

विसृज्य सशरं चापं शोकसंविग्नमानसः ।। (I-47) ।।

"Sanjay is narrating the events to king Dhritrashtra, he says "O king at this point Arjun comes down from the chariot keeps his bow and arrows on the ground. He is very sad, full of remorse, pessimistic and demoralised, to see the events unfolding in front of him. He has decided not to fight at any cost."

CHAPTER II

Arjun is Very Sad. He does not Want to fight and Lord Krishna is giving Advice to Him

तं तथा कृपयाविष्टमश्रुपूर्णाकुलेक्षणम् ।
विषीदन्तमिदं वाक्यमुवाच मधुसूदनः ।। (II-1) ।।

Sanjay is explaining the events unfolding at the battle field of Kurukshetra. He says "O king, Arjun is very sad, demoralised and in a state of shock. When Krishna sees this he goes near Arjun and tries to explain the situation so that he comes out of sadness and confusion."

कुतस्त्वा कश्मलमिदं विषमे समुपस्थितम् ।
अनार्यजुष्टमस्वर्ग्यकीर्तिकरं अर्जुन ।। (II-2) ।।

Krishna is surprised at the attitude of Arjun at this time just before the starting of the war. He says "Why are you behaving like a coward? This does not behold well for a warrior. It will only give disrespect to you and your family. Therefore you must behave like a warrior and go ahead for the challenge."

क्लैब्यं मा स्म गमः पार्थ नैतत्त्वय्युपपद्यते ।
क्षुद्रं हृदयदौर्बल्यं त्यक्त्वोत्तिष्ठ परंतप ।। (II-3) ।।

Krishna syas. "O Arjun, you should not be weak at heart as this stage. This will only bring disrespect to you and your family. You should have control on body and mind. Therefore you should get ready for the battle."

कथं भीष्ममहं संख्ये द्रोणां च मधसूदन ।
इषुभिः प्रतियोत्स्यामि पूजार्हावरिसूदन ।। (II-4) ।।

Arjun replies to Krishna "O Madhusudana how can I kill my grand father Bhishma and my own teacher Dronacharya? Both of them are my elders, most respected and loved ones. I cannot even dream of killing my most dear elders. Therefore, I will not pick up my bow against these people at any cost."

गुरूनहत्वा हि महानुभावान् श्रेयो। भोक्तुं भैक्ष्यमपीह लोके ।
हत्वार्थकामांस्तु गुरूनिहैव भुंजीय भोगान् रूधिरप्रदिग्धान् ।। (II-5) ।।

"O Krishna I will prefer to beg for living but will not do any harm to any elders *i.e.*, Pitamah Bhishma and our guru Dhronacharya. I will not accept those riches which are soaked in the blood of my elders."

This shows the love and respect Arjun had for his grand father Bhishma and teacher Drona. He is not ready to kill his elders at any cost.

न चैतद्विद्म: कतरन्नो गरीयो यद्वा जयेम यदि वा नो जयेयु: ।
यानेव हत्वा न जिजीविषामस्तेऽवस्थिता: प्रमुखे धार्तराष्ट्रा: ।। (II-6) ।।

Arjun says "O Krishna we do not know if we are going to win this battle or the sons of Dhritarashta are going to defeat us. I do not wish to kill them I do not wish to live by killing them, even if they are standing in front of me for war."

कार्पण्यदोषोपहतस्वभाव: पृच्छमि त्वां धर्मसम्मूढचेता: ।
यच्छ्रेय: स्यान्निश्चिंत ब्रूहि तन्मे शिष्चस्तेऽहं शाधि मां त्वां प्रपन्नम् ।। (II-7) ।।

Arjun says to Krishna "I feel myself very weak and unable to take any decision for or against the war. I am confused and do not know as to which way to go in the present circumstances. O Krishna, I am your disciple and I request you to show me the right path."

As Arjun's mind is vacillating is extremely demoralized and confused at this stage. He had a great faith in Krishna, therefore he requests for guidance. He was sure that the Lord will show him the correct path in these circumstances.

नहि प्रपश्यामि ममापनुद्या यच्छो। कमुच्छोषणमिन्द्रियाणम।
अवाप्य भूमावसपत्नमृद्धराज्यं सुराणामपि चाधिपत्यम् ।। (II-8) ।।

Arjun says "O Krishna inspite of the fact that I am a king and very powerful, but still am feeling very weak and powerless. My mind is in confused state and unable to give me any definite direction. Therefore I request you (Lord Krishna) to help me come out of this confusion."

Arjun is in confused state of mind, he does not know whether to fight or not to therefore, he wants the guidance of Lord Krishna so that he could decide regarding the war.

एवमुक्त्वा हृषीकेशं गुडाकेशः परंतप ।
न योत्स्य इति गोविन्दमुक्त्वा तूष्णीं बभूव ह ।। (II-9) ।।

Sanjay is narrating the events unfolding at the battle field at Kurukshetra to king Dhritrashtra. He says "O king at this point Arjun keeps aside his bow and arrows and tells Krishna that he (Arjun) will not fight under these circumstances. Arjun is extremely sad, sits on the ground dejected and in a very pensive state of mind."

तमुवाच हृषीकेशः प्रहसन्निव भारत ।
सेनयोरूभयोर्मध्ये विषीदन्तमिदं वचः ।। (II-10) ।।

Sanjay says "O King Dhritarashtra, seeing Arjun in sad state of mind, Krishna speaks to him.

अशोच्यानन्वशोचस्त्वं प्रज्ञावादांश्च भाषसे ।
गतासूनगतासूंश्च नानुशोचन्ति पण्डिताः ।। (II-11) ।।

Krishna says "O Parth you are a wise and learned person and it is not good to grieve at this stage. There is no use grieving for those who are dead or those who are going to die. Therefore you should not feel sorry for those wicked people standing in front of you." Here Krishna wanted Arjun to understand that the war is being pushed by Kauravas, as such they are wicked people and Arjun should not feel sorry for them.

न त्वेवाहं जातु नासं न त्वं नेमे जनाधिपाः ।
न चैव न भविष्यामः सर्वे वयमतः परम् ।। (II-12) ।।

Krishna says "O Arjun, the cycle of life and death is an ongoing cycle and is a continuous process. You are coming in this world and going back with the time. Time is a rat which cuts the thread of life. You and me were present yesterday and will also be present in future. Similarly all these kings and warriors were present in the past and will be present in the future as well. Therefore, grieving on this account is ignorance."

"The soul never dies as such you should not have any worry for them at all."

देहिनोऽस्मिन् यथा देहे कौमार यौवनं जरा ।
तथा देहान्तर प्राप्तिर्धी रस्तत्र न मुह्यति ॥ (II-13) ॥

"O Parth our soul goes through many stages of transformation. The child is born, becomes young and then reaches old age and dies. This cycle goes on and on. He takes birth again and passes through the same cycle. As the soul never dies as such you should not feel sad for the coming battle with the Kauravas."

Here the Lord assures Arjun about the body and soul. He tells him that the body dies but the soul is permanent and never dies. Therefore there should be no cause of worry.

मात्रास्पर्शास्तु कौन्तेय शीतोष्णसुखदु:खदा: ।
आगमापायिनोऽनित्यास्तांस्तितिक्षस्व भारत ॥ (II-14) ॥

Krishna says "O son of Kunti (Arjun), The body and material pleasures are like hot and cold seasons. They come and go, this is a regular process you should not give importance to this. Therefore, you should look them as, is this is the reality."

यं हि न व्यथयंन्त्येते पुरूष पुरूषर्षभ ।
समदु:खसुखं धीरं सोऽमृतत्वाय कल्पेत ॥ (II-15) ॥

"O Arjun a person who accepts happiness and unhappiness in the same spirit, attains salvation. A person should accept what comes in his share by destiny. He should not he very happy or sad and take them as the gift of God."

नासतो विद्यते भावो नाभावो विद्यते सत: ।
अभयोरपि द्रष्टोऽन्तस्त्वनयोस्तत्त्वदर्शिभि: ॥ (II-16) ॥

"O Arjun which is false or untrue is going to perish in any case. It is only the truth which is victorious in the end.

Therefore, which is untrue that has to perish and only truth will prevail. The wise man knows what is true and what is false and takes the action accordingly."

In other words the Lord tells Arjun that he is with the truth and the Kauravas are not true and he has to decide in that spirit alone.

अविनाशि तु तद्विद्धि येन सर्वमिंद ततम् ।
विनाशमव्ययस्यास्य न कश्चित्कर्तुमर्हति ।। (II-17) ।।
अन्तवन्त इमे देहा नित्यस्योक्ताः शरीरिणः ।
अनाशिनोऽप्रेमयस्य तस्माद्युध्यस्व भारत ।। (II-18) ।।

Krishna says to Arjun "This body destroys with time, but the soul is immortal and no one can destroy it. Therefore, you should not worry for this body. No one can destroy the soul because the same cannot die. As such you should not have any doubts and prepare yourself for the battle."

य एनं वेत्ति हन्तारं यश्चैनं मन्यते हतम् ।
उभौ तौ न विजनितो नायं हन्ति न हन्यते ।। (II-19) ।।

"O Arjun a person who thinks that the soul can be destroyed or the same is mortal, that person is ignorant. The reality is the opposite. It is immortal and cannot be destroyed."

The Lord is explaining to Arjun that the soul is immortal and it is only our body which undergoes transformation *i.e.*, dies. Therefore he should not worry for this mortal body, as change is the law of nature. Neither this body is ours, nor we belong to the body. It is composed of fire, water, air, earth and ethereal fluid and will dissolve into these. But the soul is immontal. It neither takes birth nor it dies.

न जायते म्रियते वा कदाचिंन्नायं भूत्वा भविता वा न भूयः ।
अजो नित्यः शाश्वतोऽयं पुराणो न हन्यते हन्यमाने शरीरे ।। (II-20) ।।
वेदा-विनाशिनं नित्य य एनमजमव्ययम् ।
कथं स पुरूषः पार्थ कं घातयति हन्ति कम् ।। (II-21) ।।

Krishna says "O Parth the soul is immortal. Neither it takes birth nor it dies. It is our body which is taking birth again and again and dies. So you should not feel disturbed on this subject anymore. Therefore you should not have any worry on this account, you should get ready for the battle without any negative attitude and hesitation."

Krishna is reminding Arjun that the soul is immortal. By putting these thoughts in Arjun's mind the Lord wants to ensure him, so that he gets ready for the battle. Without any fear, reservations and with a positive mind.

वासांसि जीर्णानि यथा विहाय नवानि गृहणाति नरोऽपराणि ।
तथा शरीराणि विहाय जीर्णान्यन्यानि संयाति नवानि देही ।। (II-22) ।।

"As a person discards his old cloths and wear new one. In the same way the soul discards the old and worn out body and accepts a new one. It is an going process and soul keeps on going from one body to another."

नैन छिन्दन्ति शस्त्राणि नैन दहति पावकः ।
न चैनं क्लेदयन्त्यापो न शोषयति मारूत ।। (II-22) ।।

"No weapon can destroy the soul, water cannot wet it. The air cannot dry it. In other words, it is the body of the person which dies and not the soul as it indestructible"

अछेद्योऽयमदाहयोऽयमक्लेद्योऽशोष्य एव च ।
नित्यः सर्वगतः स्थाणुरचलोऽयं सनातनः ।। (II-24) ।।

O Arjun says Krishna "The soul is eternal, indestructible, unbreakable. It is omnipresent, permanent immortal and present all the time in manifest (body) or in unmanifest state. When the soul cannot be destroyed then why to worry?"

अव्यक्तोऽयमचिन्त्योऽयमविकार्योऽयमुच्यते ।
तस्मादेवं विदित्वैनं नानुशोचितुममर्हसि ।। (II-25) ।।
अथ चैनं नित्यजातं नित्यं वा मन्यसे मृतम् ।
तथापि त्वं महाबाहो नैवं शोचितुमर्हसि ।। (II-26) ।।

Krishna says "O Parth you should know that the soul is immortal, therefore you should not feel sorry or sad. So to worry about this body is without any meaning."

जातस्य हि ध्रुवो मृत्युर्ध्रुवं जन्म मृतस्य च ।
तस्मादपरिहार्येऽर्थे न त्वं शोचितुर्महसि ।। (II-27) ।।

"O Arjun one who is born is sure to die one day. Similarly one who dies will also return and born again. Therefore, it is ignorance to worry on this subject. When it is sure that one who dies will come back and vice versa then why to grieve at all? it becomes meaningless and without any foundation."

अव्यक्तादीनि भूतानि व्यक्तमध्यानि भारत ।
अव्यक्तनिधनान्येव तत्र का परिदेवना ।। (II-28) ।।

Krishna says "O Arjun before one is born it is in the unmanifest state *i.e.*, without body and after death again it is in the unmanifest state *i.e.*, without body. So the state of manifest is very short. We mostly remain in the unmanifest state *i.e.* in soul form. Then why to grieve for this at all?"

आश्चर्यवत्पश्यति कश्चिदेनमाश्चर्यवद्वदति तथैव चान्यः ।
आश्चर्यवच्चैनमन्यः शृणोति श्रुत्वाप्येनं वेद न चैव कश्चित् ।। (II-29) ।।

O Arjun the knowledge of soul is very difficult to understand. Many try to learn it but a very few can grasp it, as the same is very deep rooted. Some are even surprised with the soul knowledge.

देही नित्यमवध्योऽयं देहे सर्वस्य भारत ।
तस्मात्सर्वाणि भूतानी न त्वं शोचितुमर्हसि ।। (II-30) ।।

"O Arjun the soul is immortal and cannot be destroyed with any weapon. This you must understand, therefore there is no use worrying for the same which is eternal."

स्वधर्ममपि चावेक्ष्य न विकम्पितुमर्हसि ।
धर्म्याद्धि-युद्धाच्छ्रेयोऽन्यत्क्षत्रियस्य न विद्यते ।। (II-31) ।।

"To fight for the right cause is dharma as such you should not have any hesitation to fight. The dharma of martial race is to fight for the right cause. You are Kshtriya who belong to this race as such you will have to fight for the right cause."

यद्दच्छया चोपपन्नं स्वर्गद्वारमपावृतम ।
सुखिनः क्षत्रियाः पार्थ लभन्ते युद्धमीदृशम् ॥ (II-32) ॥

Krishna says "O Parth, the war for the right cause opens the doors of heaven for such persons. Therefore, one should not lose an opportunity since it comes so rarely."

In other words the lord explains to Arjun that fight against evil is right and it opens the gates of heaven for those people who take up the challenge against the right cause to defeat the evil forces.

अथ चेत्वमिमं धर्म्यं संग्रामं न करिष्यसि ।
ततः स्वधर्मंकीर्तिं च हित्वा पापमवाप्यसि ॥ (II-33) ॥

"Now at this stage if you do not fight, you will lose the respect of your people. It will be unwise to shirk the responsibility at this point of time. It is your duty to fight against unjust and if you do not do the same you will lose reputation and respect."

अकीर्तिं चापि भूतानि कथयिष्यन्ति ते ऽव्ययाम् ।
सम्भावितस्य चाकीर्तिमर्रणादातेरिच्यते ॥ (II-34) ॥

"Not only the present generation but the subsequent coming generations as well, will not excuse you for your cowardice. You will fall in their eyes. Therefore you must make up your mind to fight."

भंयाद्रणादुपरंत मंस्यन्ते त्वां महारथाः ।
येषां च त्वं बहुमतो भूत्वा यास्यसि लाघवम् ॥ (II-35) ॥

"O Arjun the persons who look at you as a brave warrior will also look down upon you. They will consider you as a weak and indecisive character who ran away from facing the enemy. In the eyes of your followers you will become a coward and weak person."

अवाच्यवादांश्च बहून्वदिष्यन्ति तवाहिताः ।
निन्दन्तस्तव सामर्थ्यं ततो दुःखतरं नु किम् ॥ (II-36) ॥

"All your enemies will speak bad words about you and call you a weak and coward person. This will be like a death for you. As such you will not be able to bear this criticism. Therefore, I advise you not to have any negative thoughts in your mind. Throw them out and make up your mind for the battle."

हतो वा प्राप्स्यसि स्र्वग जित्वा वा भोक्ष्यसे महीम् ।
तस्मादुत्तिष्ठ कौन्तेय युद्धाय कृतनिश्चय: ॥ (II-37) ॥

Krishna says "O son of Kunti in case you die in the battle field you will go to the heaven as martyr, and if you win then you have so many good things to enjoy on this earth. I do not have any doubt about it. So you should make up your mind for the battle, because it is positive both ways whether you win or lose."

सुखदु:खे समे कृत्वा लाभालाभौ जयाजयौ ।
ततो युद्धाय युज्यस्व नैवं पापमवाप्स्यसि ॥ (II-38) ॥

"Happiness or unhappiness, profit or loss, victory or defeat these things are immeterial in war. One should not get upset by them at all. These things do not have any importance at this point of time. So go in the battle field with an open mind. This war is not sinful because it is being fought for the right cause."

एषा ते ऽभिहिता सांख्ये बुद्धिर्योगे त्विमां शृणु ।
बुद्धया युक्तो यया पार्थ कर्मबंध प्रहास्यसि ॥ (II-39) ॥

"O Parth (Arjun) god has given us intelligence to gain knowledge. We do different deeds with its use. This intelligence should be applied by you in deeds and you will come out of the bonds you are carrying with you. Once you are clear in your mind about the path you have to take then you can keep aside all types of bondages and attachments."

नेहाभिक्रमनाशोऽस्ति प्रत्यवायो न विद्यिते ।
स्वल्पमप्यस्य धर्मस्य त्रायते महतो भयात् ॥ (II-40) ॥
व्यवसायात्मिका बुद्धिरेकेह कुरूनन्दन ।
बहुशाखा ह्यनन्ताश्च बुद्धयोऽव्यवसायिनाम् ॥ (II-41) ॥

Krishna says "O Arjun the deed done by a person never gets destroyed. The result of the same is sure. Whatever deed is done the consequence is a must. The Karma (deed) done by an individual protects him from defeat and from the cycle of deaths and births. On the path of Karma the mind is concentrated on the objective as such it remains pure. But those persons who are fickle minded, ignorant and weak minded they always end in disappointment."

यामिमा पुष्पितां वाचं प्रवदन्त्यविपश्चितः ।
वेदवादरताः पार्थ नान्यदस्तीति वादिनः ।। (II-42) ।।

"O Parth those who are immersed in the worldly pleasures and at the same time express faith in the Vedas, rituals, etc. they are the persons who are travelling in two boats at the same time.

कामात्मानः स्वर्गपरा जन्मकर्मफलप्रदाम् ।
क्रियाविशेषबहुलां भौगेश्वर्वगति प्रति ।। (II-43) ।।

"Those persons who believe in pursuing to attain heaven at all costs, they are ignorant due to this, they think of such things only. That shows the inner weakness of these people."

भोगैश्वर्वयप्रसक्तानां तयापहृतचेतसाम् ।
व्यवसायात्मिका बुद्धिः समाधौ न विधीयते ।। (II-44) ।।

"Those who have engrossed themselves in the pleasures of life only, they spoil not only the present but the future of their lives as well. Their conscious suffer from lack of confidence and resolve so they are unable to take any positive decision in life."

The person should have clear objective in mind and pursue the same with determination, courage and positive attitude.

त्रैगुण्यविषया वेदा निस्त्रैगुण्यो भवार्जुन ।
निर्द्वन्द्वो नित्यसत्त्वस्थो निर्योगक्षेम आत्मवान् ।। (II-45) ।।

"O Arjun, The Vedas explain to us the three most important things *i.e.*, nobility, pleasures of life and sins. So we should look towards them and take path of truth and nobility and avoid negative things in life. We should have confidence in God and do our routine duties in life avoiding sinful acts and deceit. Our thoughts should be pure and in the pursuit of God we should try to remain on the side of truth and fair play. Leading such life takes one towards, nobility and in the final run to Almighty."

यावानर्थ उदपाने सर्वतः संप्लुतोदके ।
तावान् सर्वेषु वेदेषु ब्राह्मणस्य विजानतः ।। (II-46) ।।

"A person who has attained God he becomes wise and calm. The worldly treasures become secondary. He is like a person who has seen the ocean, then the importance of ponds become insignificiant for him. Similarly, when a person is near the God, other pleasues of life become of no value to him."

कर्मण्येवाधिकारस्ते मा फलेषु कदाचन ।
मा कर्मफलहेतुर्भूर्मा ते संगोऽस्त्वकर्मणि ।। (II-47) ।।

"Keep on doing your duties and do not bother for the results. Do not unnecessarily worry regarding the consequences of your actions. Your sole duty is to do Karma (duty) and leave the rest to the Almighty. He is there to look after you. Only efforts are required from your side. The results of those actions is in the hands of God."

But this does not mean that one should not strive for action or not to work or not to take those actions to their logical conclusions. One must keep up doing efforts and the results will definitely come in the positive. Keep on moving ahead towards your goal in life and the results are sure to come in your favour. God will definitely show the right path, and ultimately contentment and salvation. Have faith in Him and carry on with the work, success is bound to come in due course of time.

योगस्थः कुरू कर्माणि संगं त्यक्त्वा धनंजय ।
सिद्धयसिद्धयोः समो भूत्वा समंत्व योग उच्यते ।। (II-48) ।।

Krishna says "O Dhananjaya (Arjun) keep on doing your duties regardless of success or failure. Do not keep negative thoughts in your mind. Do not desire for the results of those actions. Your duty is foremost and keep it in mind. Leave rest in the hands of God."

दूरेण ह्यवरं कर्म बुद्धियोगाद्धनंजय ।
बुद्धौ शरणमन्विच्छ कृपणाः फलहेतवः ।। (II-49) ।।

"O Arjun when you do any deed (Karma) and expect results or beg for some favour then you can he compared to a beggar. So do not expect any favour for your actions. Your duty is to do Karma and leave the rest in His hands. You should not desire for favour because God is in the knowledge of all what is happening, and He will definitely come for your rescue."

बुद्धियुक्तो जहातीह उभे सुकृतदुष्कृते ।
तस्माद्योगाय युज्यस्व योगः कर्मसु कौशलम् ।। (II-50) ।।

"A pure soul always does pure deeds and leave them here in the world when he passes away. He does not want to keep them for himself. Therefore self sacrifice is one of the finest deeds. Do good deeds and leave them without desiring any results, to be judged by the others."

कर्मजं बुद्धियुक्ता हि फलं त्यक्त्वा मनीषिणः ।
जन्मबन्धविनिर्मुक्ताः पदं गच्छन्त्यनामयम ।। (II-51) ।।

"O Arjun these types of pious souls leave everything and achieve salvation. They free themselves from worldly bonds and unite with the Supreme. Achieve Mokshya and freedom. They come out the cycle of birth and deaths and reside in heaven."

यदा ते मोहकलिलं बुद्धिर्व्यतितरिष्यति ।
तदा गन्तासि निर्वेदं श्रोतव्यस्य श्रुतस्य च ।। (II-52) ।।

Krishna says "O Arjun when a person comes out from the attachments, he attains peace of mind. With this detachment from the worldly attractions he gets above the desires, and away from all the bondages of life. He becomes pious."

"When you do not think of profit or loss, happiness and unhappiness you become indifferent to all the materialistic things. At this stage he attains salvation and ready for the heavenly journey."

श्रुतिविप्रतिपन्ना ते यदा स्थास्यति निश्चला ।
समाधावचला बुद्धिस्तदा योगमवाप्स्यसि ।। (II-53) ।।

"O Arjun your mind will get stabilized and you will be able to unite yourself with God. A person becomes confused by listening to various types of voices in the world. With a stable mind you will get peace and attain Mokshya or salvation."

The Lord is explaining to Arjun about getting peace of mind. He tells him to follow the path shown by God to get the same. Arjun is restless and confused and the Lord is trying to calm him down so that he comes out of his misgivings.

स्थितप्रज्ञस्य का भाषा समाधिस्थस्य केशव ।
स्थितधीः किं प्रभाषेत किमासीत व्रजेत किम् ।। (II-54) ।।

O Keshava (Krishna) Arjun asks "O Lord please let me know the signs of a person who has attained salvation (Mokshya), as to how he looks and how can he be identified."

After listening to Lord Krishna Arjun becomes interested as to how a person can become peaceful at mind, in a state of calm and tranquility. Arjun is very much confused and funds himself helpless, in a state of despair. He wants to know from the Lord as to how to attain peace of mind and happiness in life.

"प्रजहाति यदा कामान्सर्वान्पार्थ मनोगतान् ।
आत्मन्येवात्मना तुष्टः स्थितप्रज्ञस्तदोच्यते ।। (II-55) ।।

Krishna says "O Parth (Arjun) a person who discards desires and expectations becomes perfect. Because the worldly attractions at this point do not get the upper hand now. At this stage a person becomes peaceful and calm in his approach."

Krishna was able to calm down Arjun by his words. Arjun had become very restless and the Lord was successful because Arjun was very much disturbed in the battle field. He is no more engulfed by the negative feelings in his mind and thus becomes calm.

दु:खेष्वनुद्विग्नमना: सुखेषु विगतस्पृह: ।
वीतरागभयक्रोध: सिथतधीर्मुनिरूच्यते ।। (II-56) ।।

"A person who remains calm in happiness or unhappiness is a perfect man. He is not disturbed by the positives or the negatives situations in life. Such a person remains steady in the ups and downs of life. Lust, anger, attachments, greed, pride etc. cannot deviate him from the right path. He is a perfect man because his mind is calm and stable. Therefore he becomes a pious person."

य: सर्वत्रान् भिस्तेहस्तत्तत्प्राप्य शुभाशुभम् ।
नभिनन्दति न द्वेष्टि तस्य प्रज्ञा प्रतिष्ठिता ।। (II-57) ।।

"A person who is stable in mind, success or failure, happiness or unhappiness are equal to him. He may get pleasant or unpleasant things in his life but does not lose his balance and keeps himself calm in his life. He always looks towards positive side of the problems. He is perfect man and these attributes lead him to salvation or Mokshya."

यदा संहरते चायं कूर्मोऽङगानीव सर्वश: ।
इन्द्रियाणीन्द्रियार्थेभ्यस्तस्य प्रज्ञा प्रतिष्ठिता ।। (II-58) ।।

"O Arjun a stable person is just like a turtle, who withdraws all its organs and takes them inside the shell. Similarly a pious and stabilized person also withdraws the tendencies like lust, anger, greed, attachment, ego, fear, hatred etc. inside his body and does not allow them to rule over him."

विषया विनिवर्तन्ते निराहारस्य देहिन: ।
रसवर्ज रसोऽप्यस्य परं दृष्ट्वा निवर्तते ।। (II-59) ।।

"When a person detaches himself from all the worldly attractions and tendencies *i.e.*, lust, anger, greed, attachments, ego, fear and hatred he becomes a sacred and holy person. But still sometimes "desires" remain inside. As the person reaches near God, these also vanish with the time. At this stage a person experiences signs of salvation or Mokshya."

यततो ह्यापि कौन्तेय पुरूषस्य विपश्चितः ।
इन्द्रियाणि प्रमाथीनि हरन्ति प्रसभं मनः ।। (II-60) ।।

Lord Krishna says "O son of Kunti, if a person is unable to witdraw himself from the carnal tendencies, he is unable to control himself from getting sinful. The control over them leads towards contentment, pleasant state of mind, happiness and devoid of all the desires and worries. He experiences a new type of inner strength and courage. His thoughts become pure and he does not harm anyone in life.

His actions are positive and he is able to transform others with his actions and thoughts."

तानि सर्वाणि सयंम्य युक्त आसीत मत्परः ।
वशे हि यस्येन्द्रियाणि तस्य प्रज्ञा प्रतिष्ठिता ।। (II-61) ।।

Lord Krishna says "O Arjun a person who wants to attain Me (God) should have control on his sensory organs, must be away from the carnal tendencies of lust, anger, greed, attachments, ego, hatred, desires, etc. One who is above all these things will attain Me (God)."

This is the advice given by Lord Krishna to Arjun. Though it looks very light, but in actual practice it is most difficult to keep away from all the above tendencies. The person who is able to conquer them is definitely is a divine soul and leads himself towards salvation *i.e.*, Mokshya.

ध्यायतो विषयान्पुंसः संङ्गस्तेषूपजायते ।
सङ्गात्सञ्जायते कामः कामात्क्रोधाऽभिजायते ।। (II-62) ।।
क्रोधाभ्दवति स्ममोहः स्ममोहातस्मृति विभ्रमः ।
स्मृति भ्रमशाद्बुद्धिनाशो बुद्धिनाशात्प्रणश्यति ।। (II-63) ।।

"O Arjun when a person gives freedom to desires he starts thinking to attain them. But when he is unable to fulfil them anger is born in the mind. This leads to restlessness and confused memory. In anger and confused state of mind he is unable to take right decisions. With the result he keeps on making wrong and harmful decisions."

Lord tells Arjun to have a check on desires, because there is no end of the same. One leads to other and the process continues. Desires are like sugar in a cup of milk. If we put a spoon, it is drinkable, but if we put four or five spoons in the same cup, we are unable to drink it. Similarly, in the cup of life if we put plenty of desires its become unbearable and we are in unhappy frame of mind. But if the quantity of desires is less, we will find ourself happy and full of positive energy. We ourselves will be happy and spread the same all around us.

रागद्वेषवियुक्तैस्तु विषयानिन्द्रियै श्चरन् ।
आत्मवश्यैर्विधेयात्मा प्रसादमधिगच्छति ।। (II-64) ।।
प्रसादे सर्वदुःखांना हानिरस्योपजायते ।
प्रसन्नचेतसो ह्याशु ति। बुद्धिः पर्यवतिष्ठति ।। (II-65) ।।

"O Arjun a person who has detached himself from all the attachments in life, leads it with contentment, happiness and in the positive frame of mind. He is away from the pains and pleasures. His mind is full of confidence and positive energy. Gains and losses do not matter to him as he is far beyond these worldy things. With pure mind and thoughts he is always near the God. He is always in the happy frame of mind and faces the world with confidence, positive attitude."

नास्ति बुद्धिरयुक्तस्य न चायुक्तस्य भावना ।
न चाभावयतः शान्तिरशान्तस्य कुतः सुखम् ।। (II-66) ।।

Krishna says "O Arjun a person who is not in control of his senses, he goes astray. He is not at peace with himself. If the mind is not under control, the person is unable to face the challenges of life and remain restless and unhappy. Such type of people cannot make any positive contribution in the life, as he himself is weak and directionless. How then can he show path to others?"

The Lord is explaining to Arjun, that a person must remain in the state of calm and peaceful atmosphere and away from the desires and other negative attractions.

इन्द्रियाणां हि चरतां यन्मनोऽनुविधीयते ।
तदस्य हरति प्रज्ञां वायुर्नावमिवाम्भसि ।। (II-67) ।।

"O Arjun as the strong wind takes over the boat and takes it in any direction with its current, similarly a person in the grip of negative tendencies *i.e.*, lust, anger, greed, attachments, ego, hatred etc. is drawn towards the road of destruction. He becomes helpless and is totally in the control of these negative forces. Therefore a person should try to remain away from these tendencies as far as possible."

The total break however is not possible, so whatever is achieved should be welcomed. The Lord tries to explain to Arjun that negative tendencies always try to enslave a person, but he should endeavour to free himself from them, to achieve victory and contentment in life.

तस्माद्यस्य महाबाहो निगृहीतानि सर्वशः ।
इन्द्रियाणीन्द्रियार्थेभ्यस्तस्य प्रज्ञा प्रतिष्ठता ।। (II-68) ।।

Lord Krishna says "O Arjun a person who has thus controlled over the evil forces, he is the perfect man. He is not effected by these forces any more because of his inner strength. He is much above the others and attain total peace of mind and the ups and downs of life do not disturb him anymore."

या निशा सर्वभूतानां तस्यां जागर्ति संयमी ।
यस्यां जाग्रति भूतानि सा निशा पश्यतो मुनेः ।। (II-69) ।।

"When an ordinary person is sleeping, it is the day time for the spiritual man, a yogi is awake at this time and is in the pursuit of knowledge."

आपूर्यमाणमचलप्रतिष्ठं समुद्रमापः प्रविशन्ति यद्वत् ।
तद्वत्कामा यं प्रविशन्ति सर्वे शान्तिमाप्नोति न कामकामी ।। (II-70) ।।

"O Arjun just as the water of river joins the ocean without making any noise, in the same way the sinful tendencies are absorbed by a noble person and they are unable to corrupt him. As the ocean embraces all the rivers coming to it, in the same way a noble person is able to absorb all the tendencies in him without being corrupted."

विहाय कामान्यः सर्वान्पु मां श्चशी निःस्पृहः ।
निर्ममो निरहङ्कारः स शान्तिमधि गच्छति ॥ (II-71) ॥

"The person who has renounced the evil tendencies of lust, anger, greed, attachment, ego, fear etc. attains salvation or Mokshya."

एषा ब्राह्मी स्थितिः पार्थ नैनां प्राप्य विमुह्यति ।
स्थित्वास्यामन्तकालेऽपि ब्रह्मनिर्वाणमृच्छति ॥ (II-72) ॥

"O Parth (Arjun) the person who attains this at any stage he becomes one with Almighty The worldly attractions do not effect him any more. He gets freed from all the attractions of life and attains Mokshya or Salvation." In this chapter lord is trying to calm down Arjun by telling him the difference between body and soul and that soul is immortal whereas body eventually dissolves in essential elements. Lord is also advocating a path of Rational Detachment, yet doing your Karma, *i.e.* Treating all our possessions as TRUST PROPERTY given by God as whatever we have was someone's else yesterday and will be someone else tomorrow, whatever we have, we have taken from God, we have come empty handed and go the same way. So only detached Karma leads to Salvation and eternal bliss.

CHAPTER III

Lord Krishna is Telling Regarding Gyan Yoga and Karam Yoga. One is followed by Saints and Yogis while the Latter is followed by others in General

ज्यायसी चेत्कर्मणस्ते मता बुद्धिर्जनार्दन ।
तत्किं कर्मणि घोरे मां नियोजयसि केशव ।। (III-1) ।।

Arjun asks Krishna, "O Lord, why you want me to fight with Kaurvas? Why to go to war at all? You yourself have given more importance to wisdom over deeds. These two things are contradicting each other. On the one side you are asking me to use wisdom and at the same time you are saying to do deeds (war). These two are opposite to each other. I am confused as to which path to choose?"

"Therefore I am in two minds whether to fight or not. Please show me the correct direction because my wisdom says that this war is not good, neither for us nor for the Kaurvas (our cousins). O Lord please explain and guide."

व्यामिश्रेणेव वाक्येन बुद्धिं मोहयसीव मे ।।
तदेकं वद निश्चित्य येन श्रेयोऽहमाप्नुयाम् ।। (III-2) ।।

"O Lord, you are confusing me by giving contradictory opinions. On the one hand you are asking to use wisdom and at the same time you are asking to do deed (Karma) and fight. These two are opposite to each other. Please explain because I am confused. Therefore let me know the right path from the two *i.e.*, wisdom or deed (duty), because my wisdom says that we should not go to war with Kauravas."

लोकेऽस्मिन्द्विविधा निष्ठा पुरा प्रोक्ता मयानघ ।
ज्ञानयोगेन साङ्ख्यानां कर्मयोगेन योगिनाम् ।। (III-3) ।।

"O Arjun there are two paths enunciated by God for the people to follow. One is *Gyan Yoga* or the path which is followed by the spiritual scholars (Saints) and the other is *Karam Yoga* which is followed by deed seekers. The rishis and sages they follow the Gyan Yoga path and the other the latter *i.e. Karam Yoga*, that means doing the duty or action during the course of one's life."

न कर्मणामनारम्भान्नैष्कर्म्य पुरूषोऽश्नुते ।
न च संन्यसनादेव सिद्धिं समधिगच्छति ।। (III-4) ।।

न हि कश्चित्क्षणमपि जातु तिष्ठत्यकर्मकृत् ।
कार्यते ह्यवशः कर्म सर्वः प्रकृतिजैर्गुणैः ।। (III-5) ।।

"O Arjun, You cannot renounce deeds (duty) in this life. It is not necessary that if you do not do duty you will not get the spiritual wisdom. But the same can happen in the opposite direction as well. You do the deeds in life but you may not get the spiritual wisdom. Everyone has to perform some kind of Karma (duty) in his life. A person has to do some kind of duty in life. Because this is the law of nature and an individual cannot escape from Karma, whether he likes it or not.

कर्मेन्द्रियाणि संयम्य य आस्ते मनसा स्मरन् ।
इन्द्रियार्थान्विमूढात्मा मिथ्याचारः स उच्यते ।। (III-6) ।।
यस्त्विन्द्रियाणि मनसा नियम्यरभते अर्जुन ।
कर्मेन्द्रियै कर्मयोगमसक्तः स विशिष्यते ।। (III-7) ।।

"O Arjun a hypocrite desires all the carnal attractions but from outside shows and acts as if he does not have those tendencies. But on the other hand a pious individual is in reality away from them. He is immune to them. O Arjun the latter is the real sacred person, who has actually renounced lust, anger, greed, attachment and ego. He lives in the world at the same time away from these tendencies. He is the real Karam Yogi."

नियंत कुरू कर्म त्वं कर्म ज्यायोह्यर्कमणः ।
शरीरात्रापि च तेन प्रसिद्धयेदकर्मणः ।। (III-8) ।।
यज्ञार्थात्कर्मणोऽन्यत्र लोकोऽयं कर्मबन्धनः ।
तदर्थं कर्म कौन्तेय मुक्तसंगः समाचर ।। (III-9) ।।

"O son of Kunti, when you come on this earth, you are

bound to do Karma (deed) without it no one can escape. If you do not do the same this will lead to unrest and despair. Living idle without doing any deed is very negative action and a person grows into a weak and sorry state of mind full of negative energy and evil tendencies. Therefore a person must keep on doing his duties detached from negative forces so as to be happy in life, and remain cheerful. So remaining detached from all allurements, keep on moving and doing your duties till the end of your life.

This will give you satisfaction and contentment in life."

सहयज्ञाः प्रजाः सृष्ट्वा पुरोवाच प्रजापतिः ।

अनेन प्रसविष्यध्वमेष वोऽस्त्विष्टकामधुक् ।। (III-10) ।।

देवान्भावयतानेन ते देवा भावयन्तु व ।

परस्पंर भावयन्तः श्रेयः परमवाप्स्यथ ।। (III-11) ।।

"Lord Brahma asked his people to perform 'Yajna' to please the Gods. When they thus are happy they will reward people with peace and happiness. So perform Yajnas without any negative thoughts in your mind. This will enrich you with contentment and with a sense of fulfilment."

Lord Krishna tells Arjun the importance of performing Yajnas in ones daily life. Yajna not only purify the atmosphere but at the same time give enrichment of thoughts and a sense of satisfaction to an individual. So performing of Yajnas is very beneficial for the mankind as well as for the nature.

इष्टान्भोगान्हि वो देवा दास्यन्ते यज्ञभाविताः ।

तैर्दत्तानप्रदायैभ्यो यो भुंक्ते स्तेन एव सः ।। (III-12) ।।

"These Yajnas keep the Almighty happy and in return grants fulfilment and happiness to a person. But those who do not thank God for the things He has given to a person, such people are thankless. We must pay back to God by performing Yajnas."

यज्ञशिष्टाशिनः सन्तो मुच्यन्ते सर्वकिल्बिषैः ।

भुंजते ते त्वधं पापाये पचन्त्यात्मकारणात् ॥ (III-13) ॥

"Those people who take leftover after a Yajnas as prasad become pious and cleansed of all the sins and curses. But those people who do not perform any kind of Yajnas. do not get anything worthwhile in life."

The Lord tells Arjun that when you come in this world do something for the mankind as well, leave behind something to be remembered by the coming generations. Do good for the humanity with your positive contribution to the society.

अन्नाःद्भवन्ति भूतानि पर्जन्यादन्नसम्भवः ।
यज्ञाद्भवति पर्जन्यो यज्ञः कर्मसमुद्भवः ॥ (III-14) ॥
कर्म ब्रह्मोद्भवं विद्धि ब्रह्मक्षस्समुद्भवम ।
तस्मात्सर्वगंत ब्रह्म नित्यं यज्ञे प्रातिष्ठतम् ॥ (III-15) ॥

"Food is the life line for the people. A man or animal cannot live without it. Food is produced by water. If there is no water food cannot be grown. By performing Yajnas we help the making of rains. As the vapours created by doing Yajna go up the sky and form clouds. Thus, in turn it is converted into rain and give back water to earth. Thus the food is generated for the mankind. Therefore, performing of Yajna is very helpful. It is life for all. We find this in Vedas, they are the creater of civilization. Thus, we must respect them because they have been created by God himself for the betterment of mankind."

The Lord is explaining to Arjun regarding the importance of doing Yajnas. It is not only good for self, but for the whole universe and mankind.

एवं प्रवर्तित चक्रं नानुर्वतयतीह यः ।

अधायुरिन्द्रियारामो मोघं पार्थं स जीवति ॥ 16 ॥

यस्त्वात्मरतिरेव स्यादात्मतृप्तश्च मानवः ।

आत्मन्येव च संतुष्टस्तस्य कार्यं न विद्यते ॥ 17 ॥

"The persons who do not perform these duties towards nature are bound to repent at the latter stage. They take the share from the nature but do not reciprocate, they are sure to suffer. But this does not apply to the pious persons who are detached from all worldly attractions."

In other words, a person must pay back to nature as he accepts blessings from it. Doing Yajna is one duty to pay back to mother earth, because it is very beneficial to the universe and to the mankind.

नैव तस्य कृतेनार्थो नाकृतेनेह कश्चन ।

न चास्य सर्वभूतेषु कश्चिदर्थ व्यापाश्रय: ।। (III-18) ।।

तस्मादसक्त: सततं कार्यं कर्म समाचर ।

असक्तो ह्याचरन्कर्म परमाप्नोति पुरूष: ।। (III-19) ।।

"O Arjun a person who is away from attachments and attractions of the world, he may or may not do Yajnas. But O Arjun I will advise you to do the same and keep up doing for the betterment of self and nature. The nature has given us so many things but does not demand anything in return. Therefore, we should pay back to it as far as possible with some positive contribution."

कर्मणैव हि संसिद्धिमास्थिता जनकादय: ।
लोकसंग्रहमेवापि सम्पश्यन्कर्तुमर्हसि ।। (III-20) ।।
यद्यदाचरति श्रेष्ठस्तत्त देवेतरो जन: ।
स यत्प्रमाणं कुरूते लोकस्तदनुवर्तते ।। (III-21) ।।

Krishna says "O Arjun even King Janak (father of Sita) used to perform Yajnas. He was extremely pious and God loving person. He also performed the same without any desires or obligation. So he is saint."

"Therefore I advise you the same. A leader is always followed by others. So other will also follow your example, and do the same for the welfare of nature and humanity."

न मे पार्थास्ति कर्तव्यं त्रिषु लोकेषु किंचन ।

नानवाप्तमवाप्तव्यं वर्त एव च कर्मणि ।। (III-22) ।।

यदि ह्यहं न वर्तेय जातु कर्मण्यतन्द्रितः ।

मम वर्त्मानुवर्तन्ते मनुष्या पार्थ सर्वशः ।। (III-23) ।।

Krishna says "O Parth (Arjun) look at me, I am the creator of this universe but still I have come on this earth in human form and do deeds (Karmas) to show way to the mankind. I am the Lord of the Universe (God) but still I perform the deeds to help my people. O Arjun I am doing so that the mankind follow me and do the same for the humanity and nature. A person always follows his leader and does the same thing as done by the leader."

"Though it is not necessary for me to do all this (deed), but still I do the same so as to show the right path to the mankind for happiness and contentment."

उत्सीदेयुरिमे लोका न कुर्या कर्म चेदहम् ।

संकरस्य च कर्ता स्यामुपहन्यामिमाः प्रजाः ।। (III-24) ।।

सक्ताः कर्मण्यविद्वांसो यथा कुर्वन्ति भारत ।

कुर्याद्विद्वांस्तथासक्ता शिचकीर्षुर्लोकसंग्रहम् ।। (III-25) ।।

"O Bharat (Arjun) if I do not do the good deeds (Karmas) the man kind will become directionless and sinful. I do deeds, to give example to people, not to sit idle and do something good for the society.

"So Arjun a good and pious person must perform good Karmas to show way to others. The weak and ignorant look towards the nobles to guide them. Therefore a saintly person should be an example to the ignorants and lead them in doing positive and good deeds (Karmas) in life."

न बुद्धिभेदं जनयेदज्ञानां कर्म संगिनाम् ।

जोषयेत्सर्वकर्माणि विद्वान्युक्तः समाचरन् ।। (III-26) ।।

प्रकृतेः क्रियमाणानि गुणैः कर्माणि सर्वशः ।

अहंकार विमूढात्मा कर्तामिति मन्यते ।। (III-27) ।।

"O Arjun a wise man must help the ignorants in doing good deeds in life. In fact he should set an example to others, so that they follow him to attain salvation in life. The person who is full of ego in himself cannot get happiness.

"The learned person should help the others for the attainment of the power supreme, as is being done by sages and saints. They always give something to a person who comes to them. They are full of positive energy and sparkle the same to others. But on the other hand a person who is full of ego and pride cannot reach God or get peace of mind. A conceited man can not reach happiness and satisfaction in life."

तत्त्ववितु महाबाहो गुणकर्मविभागयोः ।
गुणा गुणेषु वर्तन्त इति मत्वा न सज्जते ।। (III-28) ।।
प्रकृतेगुर्णसम्मूढ़ाः सज्जन्ते गुणकर्मसु ।
तानकृत्स्नविदो मन्दान्कृत्स्नविन्न विचालयेत् ।। (III-29) ।।

"A wise man does not fall prey to the allurements of life and remain aloof from them. For them lust, anger, greed, attachments, ego, fear etc. are far away. They do not allow themselves to be attracted by these evil tendencies. But on the other hand a conceited man finds himself engulfed by them. A wise man must try to help such people to come out of these negative tendencies, as nothing is impossible to achieve, if one is determined to do the same. It is difficult in the beginning but with strong will and determination any person can do it. The pious and wise man should help them in every possible way."

मयि सर्वाणि कर्माणि सन्यस्याध्यत्म चेतसा ।
निराशीर्निर्ममो भूत्वा युध्यस्व विगतज्वरः ।। (III-30) ।।
ये मे मतमिंद नित्यमनुतिष्ठन्ति मानवाः ।
श्रद्धावन्तोऽनसूयन्तो मुच्यन्ते तेऽपि कर्मभिः ।। (III-31) ।।

"O Arjun a person who follows my (God) advice attains Mokshya (salvation) and unite with me. The good deeds (Karmas) done by a person help at the end of his life. The person who follows the guidelines given by saints and sages calms down, becomes happy and contented in life. He elevates himself much above the rest. The person who follows the advice of the Almighty gets liberated from the worldly attractions and leads a happy and contented life.

ये त्वेतदभ्यसूयन्तो नानुतिष्ठन्ति मे मतम् ।

सर्वज्ञानविमूढांस्तान्विद्धि नष्टानचेतसः ।। (III-32) ।।

"Those persons who do not believe in me (God) and do not follow My advice are condemned to the cycle of births and deaths. They are never happy or contented in life and wonder from one place to another in search of peace and happiness. They keep on coming and going on this earth without any purpose or direction."

सदृशं चेष्टते स्वस्याः प्रकृतेर्ज्ञानवानपि ।

प्रकृति यान्ति भूतानि निग्रहः किं करिष्यति ।। (III-33) ।।

इन्द्रियस्येन्द्रिस्यार्थे रागद्वेषौ व्यवस्थितौ ।

तयोर्न वशमागच्छेत्तौ ह्यस्य परिपन्थिनौ ।। (III-34) ।।

"All the persons in this universe are guided by their nature and inner instincts. All the actions performed by them are driven by their nature. So each person acts according to his nature or inner feelings. A person should not be captive of lust, anger, greed, attachments, ego, hatred etc. He should try to have control over them as far as possible."

श्रेयान्स्वधर्मो विगुणः परधर्मात्स्वनुष्ठितात् ।

स्वधर्मे निधनं श्रेयः परधर्मो भयावहः ।। (III-35) ।।

"O Arjun a person must follow his faith without any doubt or reservations. He who is following his own faith is much better than those who follow other's faith. A person must remain in his own faith in which he is born.

Here a question arises to which faith the Lord is talking about? The present religions except Hinduism *i.e.* Aryavarta were not born at that time. All the present other religions *i.e.* Islam, Christianity, Sikhism, Jainism, and Buddhism came much latter. We can visualize about the same only. But one thing is clear and certain that Krishna advises Arjun that each individual must try to remain in his own religion or faith and should not adopt any other faith leaving his own. Because your own faith is thousand times better than the other faith. It means in that period the other faiths, apart from Hinduism or Aryavarta must also be prevailing.

अथ केन प्रयुक्तोऽयं पापं चरति पुरूषः ।
अनिच्छन्नपि वार्ष्णेय बलादिव नियोजितः ।। (III-36) ।।

Arjun asks "O Lord Krishna inspite of not wanting, still a person does a sin. He does so many negative and harmful deeds though his conscious is against the same. Why a person goes astray? Please guide and explain this strange riddle to me."

काम एष क्रोध एष रजोगुणसमुद्भवः ।
महाशनो महापाप्मा विद्धयेनमिह वैरिणम् ।। (III-37) ।।

"Krishna tells "O Arjun desires produce sinful tendencies in a person. The excess of these sinful desires lead the person towards decline or sin. So inspite of not wanting he commits sinful acts. In order to escape from them he should have a check on his desires, so as to keep him away from the sinful acts."

धूमेनाव्रियते वह्निर्यथादर्शो मलेन च ।
यथोल्बेनावृतो गर्भस्तथा तेनेदमावृतम् ।। (III-38) ।।

"O Arjun as fire, mirror and embryo have a "Covering over them of smoke, dust and placenta in the same way wisdom of a person is covered by the dust of Kama (lust) and desires and can shine only when these coverings are removed. These coverings prevent a person from shining in life. Therefore, it is necessary to remove the covering of kama (lust) and desires from the wisdom of an individual."

"आवृतं ज्ञानमेतेन ज्ञानिनो नित्यवैरिणा ।
कामरूपेण कौन्तेय दुष्पूरेणानलेन च ।। 39 ।।

Krishna says "O son of Kunti, Kama or lust takes a person under its control. Once it has the upper hand, a person is unable to perform the other duties. Kama is like fire, both are insatiable and want more and more. So it is very imperative for a person to keep himself away from lust and desires *i.e.*, negative tendencies."

इन्द्रियाणि मनो बुद्धिरस्याधिष्ठान मुच्यते ।
एतैर्विमोहयत्येष ज्ञानमावृत्य देहिनम् ।। (III-40) ।।

"Excess of lust and desires make the person slave to these tendencies. The wisdom gets clouded and a person cannot take right decisions. So a person must have control over these sinful tendencies to shine in life." Lord says to Arjun to have control over lust, anger, greed, attachment, ego, etc.

तस्मात्त्वमिन्द्रियाण्यादौ नियम्य भरतर्षभ ।
पाप्मानं प्रजहि ह्येनं ज्ञानविज्ञाननाशनम् ।। (III-41) ।।

Lord says to Arjun "You can kill the demon of Kama in you, so that you have the upper hand, and it will not be able to cloud your wisdom and knowledge."

इन्द्रियाणि पराण्याहुरिन्द्रियेभ्यः परं मनः ।
मनसस्तु परा बुद्धिर्यो बुद्धेः परतस्तु सः ।। (III-42) ।।
एवं बुद्धे परं बुद्ध्वा संस्तभ्यात्मानमात्मना ।
जहि शत्रुं महाबाहो कामरूप दुरासदम ।। (III-43) ।।

"O Arjun you have enough strength to destroy the demon of lust. You can control the same through your mind, because it is stronger than the lustful tendencies. Above all there is your soul which can control the mind. Therefore you should not allow yourself to be controlled by Kama. You can fight it with your mind and soul."

The person who has control over his mind and soul, can achieve the highest goal in his life. By having control over sinful tendencies a person can become positive in his approach and successful in life. A person should perform his duties according to the wisdom in him and in a positive state of mind. Have check over the negative tendencies of lust, anger, greed, attachments, ego, hate, jealousy, etc.

CHAPTER IV

In this Chapter Krishna is Explaining to Arjun about the Sanyas Yoga and the Universe. How the Life Started on this Earth

In the previous chapter Lord Krishna explained to Arjun regarding Karma Yoga or duties. In the present chapter he is talking about Sanyas Yoga.

इमं विवस्वते योगं प्रोक्तवानहम व्ययम् ।
विवस्वान्मनवे प्राह मनुरिक्ष्वाकवेऽब्रवीत् ।। (IV-1) ।।

Lord Krishna says "O Arjun I (God) gave this knowledge (of the Universe or Cosmos) to the Sun in the beginning. He in turn gave the same to his son Manu, who passed on the knowledge to his son Ikshwaku. This is how it carried on."

एवं परम्पराप्राप्तमिमं राजर्षयो विदुः ।
स कालेनेह महता योगो नष्टः परन्तप ।। (IV-2) ।।

"This is how this knowledge was received by the Raj rishis. But with the span of time it disappeared from the earth."

The Lord is explaining to Arjun regarding the knowledge of the soul in the previous Chapter and here he is explaining to him about Sanyas Yoga.

स एवांय मया तेऽद्य योगः प्रोक्तः पुरातनः ।
भक्तोऽसि मे सखा चेति रहस्यं ह्येतदुत्तमम् ।। (IV-3) ।।

"O Arjun this knowledge is very secret. But I will tell you about the same because you are dear to me and have the urge of knowing, as such I give you this secret knowledge for your benefit."

अपरं भवतो जन्म परंजन्म विवस्वतः ।
कथमेतद्विजानीयां त्वमादौ प्रोक्तवा निति ।। (IV-4) ।।

Arjun was surprised at this, as to what Krishna was saying regarding the universe. He says to Krishna, "O Lord how can I believe that this knowledge was given by you to the Sun? You and me are born in this era but the Sun is there in the Cosmos from thousands of years. I am really confused and fail to understand as to what you are taking about?"

बहूनि मे व्यतीतानि जन्मानि तव चार्जुन ।
तान्यंह वेद् सर्वाणि न त्वां वेत्थ परंतप ।। (IV-5) ।।
अजोऽपि सन्नव्ययात्मा भूतानामीश्वरोऽपि सन ।
प्रकृति स्वामधिष्ठाय संभवाम्यात्ममायया ।। (IV-6) ।।

Krishna says "O Arjun it is true that you and I come on this earth again and again and it is a continuing process. But only the difference being that you do not know about the earlier births nor you will know about the future births. But I remember all these births of mine which have taken place earlier, and also have knowledge about the births which are going to take place in future as well. Though I am the protector of this universe but still I (God) come on this earth to put everything in order through my *Yogmaya*. I am eternal and there is no beginning or the end in my case."

यदा यदा ही धर्मस्य ग्लानिर्भवति भारत ।
अभ्युत्थानमधर्मस्य तदात्मानं सृजाम्यहम् ।। (IV-7) ।।
परित्राणाम् साधूनां विनाशाय च दुष्कृताम ।
धर्म संस्थापना थार्य संभवामि युगे युगे ।। (IV-8) ।।

"O Bharat (Arjun) whenever the evil forces take over the earth I (God) incarnate myself and take birth to destroy these evil forces and establish the rule of law. I manifest myself and protect the good from the evil. This has been happening and will keep on happening in future as well. From time to time I take human form and come on this earth to help the pure and pious people and teach lesson to impure and dishonest ones. O Arjun whenever crime and injustice increase manifolds and society degenerates I come on this earth to save just and pious persons from the evil forces."

There is a saying if bad days come, good days are not far behind. Similarly Lord Krishna tells Arjun that when the evil forces take over the society and the crimes reach the peak, the God comes in the shape of a human being to protect it from these evil forces.

In other words the Lord is reassuring the mankind not to worry and fight the evil forces to the utmost. So the devotee should not feel disheartened and fight the enemies with all his might as the Lord is behind him and supports him.

जन्म कर्म च मे दिव्यमेंव यो वेत्ति तत्वतः ।
त्यक्त्वा देहं पुनर्जन्मं नैति मामेति सोऽर्जुन ।। (IV-9) ।।

"O Arjun I take birth from time to time and come on this earth to establish rule of law. My births and deeds are divine. A person who has faith in Me (God) comes out the cycle of births and deaths. That person comes to me and remain under my protection thereafter."

वीतरागभयक्रोधा मन्मया मामुपाश्रिताः ।
बहवो ज्ञानतपसा पूता मभ्दावमागताः ।। (IV-10) ।।
ये यथा मां प्रपद्यन्ते तांस्तथैव भजाम्यहम् ।
मम वर्त्मानुवर्तन्ते मनुष्याः पार्थ सर्वशः ।। (IV-11) ।।

Krishna says "O Parth (Arjun) the person who has conquered the evil tendencies of lust, anger, greed, attachments, ego, jealousy, etc. in him, he becomes one of me. The person who has full faith in Me (God), I see that he is not let down in any way. One who leaves everything to Me I look after and free him from all bondages of life and death. Only the devotee should have full confidence and faith in Me."

कांक्षन्तः कर्मणां सिद्धिं यजन्त इह देवताः ।
क्षिप्रं हि मानुषे लोके सिद्धिर्भवति कर्मजा ।। (IV-12) ।।

"O Parth you should have complete faith in Me (God). The persons who worship lesser gods do reach me ultimately but it takes a longer time. Therefore you should have full confidence in Me and leave the rest and I will look after the same.

चातुर्वर्ण्यं मया सृष्टं गुणकर्मविभागशः ।
तस्य कर्तारमपि मां विद्धयकर्तारमव्ययम ।। (IV-13) ।।

"O Arjun I am the creator of the four varnas. I have (God) classified the society thus so that everyone does his duty and not interfere with each other. Though I am the creator but at the same time I am detached from them."

The four varnas the Lord talking about are (*i*) Brahmin (*ii*) Kshatriya (*iii*) Vaisha (*iv*) Shudra.

(*i*) Brahmin : Means the learned one, who teaches and shows the right path to a person. The duty of a Brahmin is to give knowledge. It is not only the religious knowledge but knowledge in all walks of life. So all the Rishi munies, our teachers and other knowledge givers come in this category. They are all Brahmins because they are learned and wise men and impart knowledge to others and show the right path. This has nothing to do with any section of society. If one is born in a Brahmin family, but does the duty of defending the country against internal or extenral enemies, he will be considered as Kshatriya and vice versa. Therefore all the rishis, scienties, scholars teachers and other knowledge givers come in the category of Brahmin.

(*ii*) Kshatriya : Those people who are defending the country from internal and external enemies are Kshatriyas. Our armed forces, police, other para defence forces, our leaders, all come in this category. They are the defender of the country and protect the society from the danger of enemies, whether internal or external, so that the public remain safe and the country progresses in peaceful environments. So they all come in the category of Kshatriyas.

(*iii*) Vaisha : They are the wealth generators of the country by doing trade and creating wealth and property for the people. Our farmers, industrial workers, companies executives all come under this. By producting wealth for the country they are enriching the society.

(*iv*) Shudra : They are the one who are serving the rest of the society with their work and services. But this does not means that a Shudra remains the same, as he is born in that caste. If he attains knowledge, educates himself and enlighten the society with his knowledge and wisdom he is definitely a Brahmin in that case.

In short, the varans have nothing to do with the caste system as prevailing in our society. This classification was purely as a social structure so that all remain busy enriching the country without interfering with one another. These four varnas have nothing to do with the caste system. It was conceived purely as a social structure.

न मां कर्माणि लिम्पन्ति न मे कर्मफले स्पृहा ।
इति मां योऽभिजानाति कर्मभिर्न स बध्यते ।। (IV-14) ।।

Krishna says "O Arjun the deeds and all allurements of the world do not attract me and I (God) am beyond all these worldly attractions. Similarly, those persons who come to Me, they also get the same benefit. People who follow the divine path they become free from all the worldly bondages and attractions. They free themselves from lust, anger, greed, attachements, ego, jealousy, etc. and attain divine blessings."

एवं ज्ञात्वा कृतं कर्म पूर्वैरपि मुमुक्षभिः ।
कुरू कर्मैव तत्मात्वं पूर्वैः पूर्वतरं कृतम ।। (IV-15) ।।

Krishna says "O Arjun in the past your ancestors have also done the same to attain salvation *i.e.*, Mokshya. Therefore I advise you to do the same as done by your ancestors *i.e.*, free yourself from the worldly allurements, and get ready to fight the enemies."

Slowly but steadily the Lord is trying to remove the doubts haunting the mind of Arjun, so that he discards cowardice and gets ready for the battle against the Kaurvas, who are standing in front of him to kill him and his army. Here there is a message for the mankind that a person should not be coward and perform the duties entrusted to him by the society.

किं कर्म किमकर्मेति कवयोऽप्यत्र मोहिताः ।
तत्ते कर्म प्रवक्ष्यामि यज्ज्ञात्वा मोक्ष्यसेऽशुभात् ।। (IV-16) ।।

"O Arjun even the wise and learned persons get confused regarding the theory of actions and inactions. I will explain to you, so that you may come out of this confusion in your mind. This will liberate you from the Karmas *i.e.*, the consequences of actions."

Krishna feels that Arjun is still not confident enough and is unable to bring himself out of the confusion to fight or not to fight. He therefore, thinks that Arjun should be given more assurance so that he is liberated fully of the doubts and comes back to clear, positive and balanced state of mind.

कर्मणो ह्यपि बोद्धव्यं बोद्धव्यं च विकर्मणः ।
अकर्मणश्च बोद्धव्यं गहना कर्मणो गतिः ।। (IV-17) ।।
कर्मण्यकर्म यः पश्येदकर्मणि च कर्म यः ।
स बुद्धिमान्मनुष्येषु स युक्तः कृत्स्नकर्म कृत् ।। (IV-18) ।।

Shri Krishna explains to Arjun "The theory of Karma (action) and akarma (non-action) must be understood, wiseman takes the action accordingly. A person who sees action in inaction and inaction in action is a wiseman. He always analyses Karma and akarma in his life and takes action as per his wisdom in a positive state of mind and heart."

यस्य सर्वे समारम्भाः कामसंल्प वर्जिताः ।
ज्ञानाग्निदग्ध कर्माणं तमाहुः पण्डितं बुधाः ।। (IV-19) ।।

"A person who has sacrificed the attractions towards lust, anger, greed, attachments, ego, jealousy etc. is a pious and learned man and is called as 'Pandit' or a scholar. All others follow him and he becomes a holy man."

We should live our life as a lotus flower. Though it lives in water from beginning to the end but the drops of water cannot remain on its leaves. Similarly a person should remain in this world as lotus in water, and remain away from the evil deeds.

त्यकत्वा कर्मफलासंग नित्यतृप्तो निराश्रयः ।
कर्मण्यभि प्रवृत्तोऽपि नैव किंचित्करोति सः ।। (IV-20) ।।

"The person who has withdrawn himself from the wordly attractions becomes an example to others. Everyone tries to follow him. He spends his time in the pursuit of knowledge and the welfare of the mankind."

The person who is always doing positive Karmas (deeds) attains happiness, satisfaction and peace in life. He does positive actions and does not wait for the rewards or expecting anything in return. He is away from lust, anger, greed, attachments, ego or jealousy and always remain positive in his approach. He only believes in Karma or action and leaves everything in the hands of Almighty.

निराशीर्यतचित्तात्मा त्यक्तसर्वपरिग्रहः ।
शरीरं केवलं कर्म कुर्वन्नाप्नोति किल्वषम् ।। (IV-21) ।।

"A person who has conquered the evil tendencies, thus becomes a Yogi, because he does not have any attachments and attractions in the world. Physically he remains in the world but spiritually he is close to God, in a state of peace and calm. No worldly attachments can bind him and he elevates himself for the journey towards heaven."

यदृच्छालाभसन्तुष्टो द्वन्द्वातीतो विमत्सरः ।
समः सिद्धावसिद्धौ च कृत्वापि न निबध्यते ।। (IV-22) ।।

"O Arjun, the persons who are not jealous of anybody, joys and sorrows do not have any meaning for them neither happy in success nor sad in failure, those people are above Karma bonds. The ups and downs of life do not disturb them. They are above all the negative or positive happenings."

गतसङ्गस्य मुक्तस्य ज्ञानावस्थितचेतसः ।
यज्ञायाचरतः कर्म समग्रं प्रविलीयते ।। (IV-23) ।।
ब्रह्मर्पणं ब्रहन हविर्ब्रह्मग्नौ ब्रह्मणा हुतम ।
ब्रह्मैव तेन गन्तव्यं ब्रह्मकर्मसमाधिना ।। (IV-24) ।।

"The person who is away from the negative or evil tendencies, he elevates himself much above the rest. He is in a state of calm, remains in the service of mankind and at the sametime discharges his worldly duties, he is a real Karma Yogi. For him performing of deeds becomes secondary. By performing Yajnas he purifies himself as well as the universe. Due to performing of Yajnas he rises to the spiritual heights, other deeds become of no consequence in his case."

दैवमेवापरे यज्ञं योगिन पर्युपासते ।
ब्रह्माग्नावपरे यज्ञं यज्ञेनैवो पजुह्वति ॥ (IV-25) ॥

"Some devotees or Yogis performed Yajnas for the worship of Almighty and some do it for self purification whatever be the motive, doing Yajnas itself is very beneficial to the mankind and nature."

श्रोत्रादीनीन्द्रियाण्यन्ये संयमाग्निषु जुह्वति ।
शब्दादीन्विषयानन्य इन्द्रियाग्निषु जुह्वति ॥ (IV-26) ॥

"The evil tendencies of lust, anger, greed, attachments, ego, jealousy are under control when one is performing the Yajna as a routine. The other devotees do it as symbolic action in the worship of God."

"Both ways it is useful."

सर्वाणीन्द्रियकर्माणि प्राणकर्माणि चापरे ।
आत्मसंयमयोगाग्नौ जह्वति ज्ञानंदीपिते ॥ (IV-27) ॥

"Some of the devotees perform Yajnas or Havans so as to have full control on their sensory organs and self confidence and gaining knowledge, whatever be the motive, performing of Yajna itself is very useful practice."

द्रव्ययज्ञास्तपोयज्ञा योगयज्ञास्तथापरे ।
स्वाध्यायज्ञानयज्ञाश्च यतयः संशितव्रताः ॥ (IV-28) ॥

"O Arjun there are many types of Yajnas. Some donate money and give in kind to needy. This is also termed as Yajna. Some resort to non-violence so as to burn evil forces within, this is also a type of Yajna. Some do the fasting as a regular practice, so as to purify the mind, soul and body."

अपाने जुह्वति प्राणं प्राणेऽपानं तथापरे ।
प्राणापान गती रूद्ध्वा प्राणायाम परायणाः ॥ 29 ॥

Krishna says "O Arjun some devotee practise by blocking breathing as a Yajna. They block inhaling and some by exhaling. Some do by Prana yama, *i.e.*, blocking inhaling as well as exhaling. They are also the kind of Yajnas."

अपरे नियताहारा: प्राणान्प्राणेषु जुह्वति ।
सर्वेऽप्येते यज्ञविदो यज्ञक्षपितकल्मषा: ।। 30 ।।

"Many Yogis or devotees resort to fasting as a Yajna. They do not take any food for days together. This is also a type of Yajna or Havan. With regular fasting they are able to cleanse the body as well as the soul."

In the above few verses Lord Krishna is explaining to Arjun, the importance of doing Yajnas. He says that different type of persons do different type of Yajnas. Some educate others to spread the light of knowledge. Some do pranayams to keep the soul and body fit, and spread the message of God to others. So the Lord shows that there are so many types of Yajnas or Havans a person can do in his life. By donations one can help the needful. Similarly if one is aiding any school with funds, he is doing Yajna of education and knowledge.

यज्ञशिष्टामृतभुजो यान्ति ब्रह्म सनातनम् ।
नायं लोकोऽस्त्ययज्ञस्य कुतोऽन्य: कुरूसत्तम ।। (IV-31) ।।
एवं बहुविधा यज्ञा वितता ब्रह्मणो मुखे ।
कर्मजान्विद्धि तान्सर्वानेवं ज्ञात्वा विमोक्ष्यसे ।। (IV-32) ।।

"O Arjun the knowledge of Yajna is like nectar "As nectar is ultimate in itself in the same way the knowledge of Yajnas is also ultimate in itself. The person performing the same gets a strange sense of happiness and satisfaction in life. But the persons who are not doing so, they do not live the life in full sense. They miss something in their lives. There is mention of the practice of Yajnas in the Vedas too."

श्रेयान्द्रव्यमयाद्यज्ञाज्ज्ञानयज्ञ: परंतप ।
सर्व कर्माखिलं पार्थ ज्ञाने परिसमाप्यते ।। (IV-33) ।।

Krishna says "O Parth (Arjun), the knowledge based Yajna is the best of the rest. Because this knowledge is supreme and it leads to positive ways of living the life."

तद्विद्धि प्रणिपातेन परिप्रश्नेन सेवया ।
उपदेक्ष्यन्ति ते ज्ञानं ज्ञानिनस्तत्त्व दर्शिन: ।। 34 ।।

"O Arjun take knowledge from those who are learned and take guidance from them because they will show you the right path to move on the journey to happiness, satisfaction and salvation in life."

In this verse Lord Krishna explains to Arjun about the importance of a teacher or Guru. He always shows the right and correct path to the student or disciple. So the importance of teacher or Guru is even more than the God himself, because through the knowledge imparted by him, the student or disciple is able to reach God.

यज्ज्ञात्वा न पुनर्मोहमेवं यास्यसि पाण्डव ।
येन भूतान्यशेषेण दक्ष्यस्यात्मन्यथो मयि ।। (IV-35) ।।
अपि चेदसि पापेभ्यः सर्वेभ्यः पापकृत्तमः ।
सर्वं ज्ञानप्लवेनैव वृजिनं सन्तरिष्यसि ।। (IV-36) ।।

"O Arjun after getting the knowledge you will not suffer from any confusion. Your mind will become clear and will have complete peace of mind. The knowledge thus gained will help you to negotiate the hurdles in life. You will reach a stage where there is complete peace and happiness. Even a sinner also gets reformed. He might have done many sins and crimes in his life, but after gaining the knowledge he can transform his life and become a saint. As he gets purified by the true knowledge thus gained."

The most vivid example of this is Valmiki, who after the transformation became saint Valmiki and wrote the epic Ramayana.

यथैधांसि समिद्धोऽग्निर्भस्मासात्कुरूते ऽर्जुन ।
ज्ञानाग्निः सर्वकर्माणि भस्मसात्कुरूते तथा ।। (IV-37) ।।
न हि ज्ञानेन सदृशं पवित्रमिंह विद्यते ।
तत्स्वंय योगसंसिद्धः कालेनात्मनि विन्दति ।। (IV-38) ।।

Krishna says "O Arjun as the fire reduces everything to ash, similarly the knowledge wipes out all the sinful tendencies and a person becomes a Yogi. He enrichs the society with his positive actions. The knowledge thus gained by a person leads him towards purity of thoughts and actions.

There is nothing like gaining knowledge, it stands lofty apart from all other actions. The knowledge leads towards happiness and satisfaction. The person leads a positive life after gaining the true knowledge."

श्रद्धावांल्लभते ज्ञानं तत्परः संयतेन्द्रियः ।
ज्ञानं लब्ध्वा परां शान्तिमचिरेणाधिगच्छति ।। (IV-39) ।।
अज्ञश्चाश्रद्धाधानश्च संशयात्मा विनश्यति ।
नायं लोकोऽस्ति न परो न सुखं संशयात्मनः ।। (IV-40) ।।

"The knowledge thus gained by an individual elevates him to great heights. A person should have confidence and direction to receive this knowledge. He frees himself from the evil forces and attractions of this world. On the other hand, one who is of suspicious nature does not believe in God, finds himself surrounded by the evil and negative forces all the time.

He cannot get any happiness or satisfaction neither in this world nor in the other. He remains restless and away from the sublime bliss."

योगसन्यंस्तकर्माणं ज्ञानसंछिन्नसंशयम् ।
आत्मवन्तं न कर्माणि निबध्नन्ति धनंजय ।। (IV-41) ।।

Krishna says "O Dhananjaya (Arjun) A person who has faith in the power Supreme (God) is able to achieve all the positives in this world. He is not bound by the Karmas any more. With wisdom and positive deeds he conquers all his negative tendencies."

तस्मादज्ञानसंभूतं हृत्स्थं ज्ञानासिनात्मनः ।
छित्त्वैनं संशयं योगमातिष्ठोत्तिष्ठ भारत ।। (IV-42) ।।

Krishna says "O Bharat (Arjun) you should cut down doubts and ignorance from your mind with the sword of wisdom and knowledge. Doubts and ignorance create confusion in the mind and the person is unable to decide with positive mind. So you should destroy them with your wisdom and knowledge and prepare for the coming battle."

CHAPTER V

Arjun is Confused and He is Unable to Make his Mind about the War with Kaurvas. He is Asking the Lord about the Sanyas Yoga and the Karam Yoga and as to which Should He Follow

संन्यासं कर्मणां कृष्ण पुनर्योगं च शंससि ।

यच्छ्रेय एतयोरेकं तन्मे ब्रूहि सुनिश्चितम् ।। (V-1) ।।

Arjun asks Krishna "O Lord on the one side you tell me to give up all desires and at the same time you talk about Karma Yoga *i.e.*, to act with wisdom and knowledge and do accordingly. They contradict each other. So please show me the correct path between the two, as I am confused thinking about the two opposing attitudes."

संन्यासं कर्मयोगश्च निःश्रेयसकरावुभौ ।

तयोस्तु कर्मसंन्यासात्कर्मयोगो विशिष्यते ।। (V-2) ।।

Krishna replies to Arjun "O Arjun as I told you earlier, there are two types of Yogas. One is Sanyas Yoga and the second is Karma Yoga. The former is practiced by saints and Yogis. They give up all the treasures of life and evolve themselves in pursuit of Almighty, this is called Sanyas Yoga. They cut themselves from the materialistic world and absorb themselves in the Godly pursuits. The latter is Karam Yogi *i.e.*, you remain in the worldly surroundings but at the sametime keep yourself attached to God. A person who is thus performing the dual duties towards God as well as to society is a Karma Yogi. So, Arjun I advise you to practice Karma Yoga in life."

In the last few verses Lord Krishna explains to Arjun about knowledge and wisdom. Armed with these a person is able to face the difficulties in life with a resolute mind and determination. The Lord has given importance to learning and knowledge. There is no age or time bar to achieve the same, provided one is inclined and has urge to obtain it. It opens the gates to reach the Almighty without it one cannot achieve anything in life. So we should try to obtain knowledge from each and every source from which it is available to us.

ज्ञेयः स नित्यसंन्यासी यो न द्वेष्टि न कांक्षति ।

निर्द्वन्द्वो हि महाबाहो सुखं बन्धात्प्रमुच्यते ।। (V-3) ।।

Krishna says, "O Arjun a person who does not harm anyone, expect nothing from any person, does not have any ill will towards anyone. He is the real Karam Yogi. Such type of persons are Godly and near to the Almighty. They do not have any desires or attachments in life. They live in this world but at the same time are not attracted by the allurements of the world. They come in the world, discharge their duties towards the society and go back to heaven. These are the attributes of a Karma Yogi."

सांख्ययोगो पृथग्बालाः प्रवदन्ति न पण्डिताः ।

एकमप्यास्थितः सम्यगुभयोर्विन्दते फलम् ।। (V-4) ।।

"O Arjun those people who do not believe in the Karam Yoga are ignorant. They feel that the Karam Yogi does not get any reward but the reality is otherwise. The person who is doing positive Karmas (deeds) are definitely rewarded by the Almighty and they come out of the bondages of this life for ever."

यत्सांख्यैः प्राप्यते स्थानं तद्योगैरपि गम्यते ।

एकं साख्यं च योगं च यः पश्यति स पश्यति ।। (V-5) ।।

Krishna says "O Arjun Gyan Yoga and Karam Yoga both are the same, as two roads meet at a point or destination. Both are rewarding in the end and the devotee reaches to the Almighty. In short, whether one follows Gyan Yoga (Sanyas Yoga) or the Karam Yoga (deeds Yoga) the final result of both is the same *i.e.*, attaining the God. But those who do not understand this they are ignorant and reach nowhere."

सन्यासस्तु महाबाहो दु:खमाप्तुमयोगत: ।
योगयुक्तो मुनिर्ब्रह्म नचिरेणाधिगच्छति ।। (V-6) ।।

"O Arjun it is extremely difficult to attain Sanyas Yoga. But a person who is able to control the negative tendencies of lust, anger, greed, attachments, ego, hatred and pride, is a Karma Yogi. Thus, with having control over these tendencies, a devotee reaches the Almighty."

योगयुक्तो विशुद्धात्मा विजितात्मा जितेन्द्रिय: ।
सर्वभूतात्मभूतात्मा कुर्वन्नपि न लिप्यते ।। (V-7) ।।

"A person who has control over the negative and evil tendencies is a pious soul. He is part and parcel of the world but at the same time away from it. He performs all the duties and at the same time doing work for the next world as well. He is a Karma Yogi."

नैव किंचित्करोमीति युक्तो मन्येत तत्ववित् ।
पश्यन्श्रृण्वन्स्पृशंजिघ्रन्नश्नन्गच्छन्स्वंपन्श्वसन ।। (V-8) ।।
प्रलपन्विसृजन्गृह्ण न्नुन्मिषन्निमिषन्नपि ।
इन्द्रियाणिन्द्रियार्थेषु वर्तन्त इति धारयन् ।। (V-9) ।।
ब्रह्मण्याधाय कर्माणि संगं त्यक्त्वा करोति य: ।
लिप्यते न स पापेन पद्मपत्रमिवाम्भसा ।। (V-10) ।।

A person knows that whatever action is being happening is due to Almighty and he himself does not have any role in the same. He is only the messenger of God. The devotee has full control on the senses, this is the sign of a Karma Yogi. He lives like the lotus flower living in the world. The lotus lives throughout in water, but if some water is put on the leaf it does not stick but falls off. Similarly a Karma Yogi lives in the world, but he does not become part of the same. So a wise person remains in the world without any attachments.

He is away from the negative tendencies of lust, anger, greed, attachments, ego, hate and jealousy. These are the attributes of a Karma Yogi.

कायेन मनसा बुद्धया केवलैरिन्द्रियैरपि ।
योगिनः कर्म कुर्वन्ति संगं त्यक्त्वात्मशुद्धये ।। (V-11) ।।

युक्तः कर्मफलं त्यक्त्वा शान्तिमाप्नोति नैष्टिकीम् ।
अयुक्तः कामकारेण फले सक्तो निबध्यते ।। (V-12) ।।
सर्वकर्माणि मनसा संन्यस्यास्ते सुखं वशी ।
नव द्वारे पुरे देही नैव कुर्वन्न कारयन् ।। (V-13) ।।

Krishna says "O Arjun such type of pious persons do only good deeds. As they are far away from vices and other negative doings. They do not harm anyone. He discharges his duties towards everyone and at the same time does not attach or bind himself with anyone. So he is near to the Almighty. He remains in a state of calm, because no worldly attraction bothers him. In the end he reaches God and leaves this world calmly and without any remorse.

न कर्तृत्व न कर्माणि लोकस्य सृजति प्रभुः ।
न कर्मफलसंयोग स्वभावस्तु प्रवर्तते ।। (V-14) ।।
नादत्ते कस्यचित्पापं न चैव सुकृतं विभुः ।
अज्ञानेनावृतं ज्ञानं तेन मुह्यन्ति जन्तवः ।। (V-15) ।।
ज्ञानेन तु तदज्ञानं येषां नाशितमात्मनः ।
तेषामादित्यवज्ज्ञानं प्रकाशयति तत्परम् ।। (V-16) ।।

"It is unwise to understand that God will take over the misfortunes or difficulties of a person. He has to undergo them as per his destiny. The name of God helps to face them with determination and self confidence. Everyone has to undergo the cycle of misfortunes as per his Karma or destiny. Therefore one should not get dishearten and accept difficulties as truth of life. He should face them with courage and self confidence. And also, this cycle keeps on changing from time to time."

When bad days come, good are not far behind. A person whose ignorance has disappeared with knowledge will reach the abode of God. The knowledge thus achieved, he can enlighten the lives of the other people as well.

तद्बुद्धयस्तदात्मानस्तन्निष्ठास्तत्परायणाः ।
गच्छन्त्यपुनरावृतिं ज्ञाननिर्धूतकल्मषाः ॥ (V-17) ॥

विद्या विनयसंपन्ने ब्राह्मणे गवि हस्तिनि ।
शुनि चैव श्वपाके च पण्डिताः समदर्शिनः ॥ (V-18) ॥
इहैव तैर्जितः सर्गो येषां साम्ये स्थितं मनः ।
निर्दोषं हि समं ब्रह्म तस्माद्ब्रह्मणि ते स्थिताः ॥ (V-19) ॥

"With gaining of kowledge a person becomes perfect. Not only his present is happy but also the next world as well. He believes in the Almighty, and the knowledge thus gained by him is utilized by him for the positive persuits and for the welfare of the mankind. He has love for all creatures living on this earth. Such type of persons are very rare and loved by God. They are away from the evil tendencies of lust, anger, greed, attachments, ego, hatred and pride, etc."

न प्रहृष्येत्प्रियं प्राप्य नोद्विजेत्प्राप्य चाप्रियम् ।
स्थिरबुद्धिरसंमूढो ब्रह्मविद्ब्रह्मणि स्थितः ॥ (V-20) ॥

"A person who is not over joyous in happiness and not extremely sorrowful in adversity is a real pious and holy man. He remains calm in the both states. He is a noble person. A person must remain in the state of calm whatever the circumstance might be. It is quite difficult to achieve this position, but with practice the same can be achieved with the time."

बाह्यस्पर्शेष्वसक्तात्मा विन्दत्यात्मनि यत्सुखम् ।
स ब्रह्मयोगयुक्तात्मा सुखमक्षयमश्नुते ॥ (V-21) ॥
ये हि संस्पर्शजा भोगा दुःखयोनय एव ते ।
आद्यन्तवन्तः कौन्तेय न तेषु रमते बुधः ॥ (V-22) ॥

Krishna says "O son of Kunti, a learned and wise person does not carve for the pleasures of life. He keeps himself busy in the positive activities entrusted to him by the society and God. He does not bind himself with the attractions in this world *i.e.*, lust, anger, greed, attachments, ego, pride or jealousy and other carnal tendencies."

शक्नोतीहैव यः सोंढु प्राक्शरीरविमोक्षणात् ।
कामक्रोधोद्भवं वेगं स युक्तः स सुखी नरः ।। (V-23) ।।

"O Arjun a person who is living in this world and at the sametime has full control over Kama (lust) and Krodha (anger) is a real Yogi *i.e.*, a pious person. As he has controlled his senses, leads a happy and contented life. He leaves the world with satisfaction."

योऽन्तः सुखोऽन्तरारामस्तथान्तर्ज्योतिरेव यः ।
स योगी ब्रह्मनिर्वाणं ब्रह्मभूतोऽधिगच्छति ।। (V-24) ।।

The person who has destroyed all desires and the other negative tendencies *i.e.*, lust, anger, greed, attachments, ego, pride and jealousy etc. is the real pure soul, *i.e.,* Yogi. God resides in such a person. As he does not have any ill will against anyone. He thus ensures for himself the road to heaven, the abode of the Almighty."

लभन्ते ब्रह्मनिर्वाणमृषयः क्षीगकल्मषा ।
छिन्नद्वैधा यतात्मानः सर्वभूतहिते रताः ।। (V-25) ।।
कामक्रोधवियुक्तानां यतीनां यतचेतसाम् ।
अभितो ब्रह्मनिर्वाणं वर्तते विदितात्मनाम् ।। (V-26) ।।

"A person who with his knowledge has controlled the evil tendencies, he attains complete peace and sublime bliss. He leads a happy and contented life."

The central idea of the above verses is the same *i.e.*, living a pure and pious life. The moral is that a person should detach himself from the carnal and negative tendencies of this world. Have positive thoughts in mind and keep on doing the duties entrusted towards the family and towards the society. When lust and anger subside, the person becomes calm and sublime. He is the real Yogi.

स्पर्शान्कृत्वा बहिर्बाह्यंश्चक्षुश्चैवान्तरे भ्रुवोः ।
प्राणापानौ समौ कृत्वा नासाभ्यन्तरचारिणौ ।। (V-27) ।।

"O Arjun some devotee do the pranayama by concentrating the thoughts in God. By bringing the eye sight and fixing it in the centre of the eyebrows and controlling inhaling and exhaling."

यतेन्द्रियमनोबुद्धिर्मुनिर्मोक्षपरायणः ।
विगतेच्छाभयक्रोधो यः सदा मुक्त एव सः ॥ (V-28) ॥

"O Arjun a person who has control over his mind, heart and senses finally gets liberated and attain Mokshya. He does not have any fear in his mind and anger can not enslave him anymore."

भोक्तारं यज्ञतपसां सर्वलोकमहेश्वरम् ।
सुहृदं सर्वभूतानां ज्ञात्वा मां शान्तिमृच्छति ॥ (V-29) ॥

"With Yajnas, penances and a pure mind the devotee reaches Me (God) ultimately. He gets peace of mind and a sense of achievement and fulfillment in his life."

In other words the Lord ensures that a devotee who comes to him with pure mind and heart gets salvation in life, and gets freedom from all bondages.

CHAPTER VI

Lord Krishna is Explaining yo Arjun About the Negative Tendencies i.e. Lust, Anger, Greed, Attachments, Pride, Ego, Jealousy etc. He is Also Telling Him About the Yoga and How to Perform it in the Right Manner

अनाश्रित: कर्मफलं कार्यं कर्म करोति य: ।

स संन्यासी च योगी च न निरग्निर्न चाक्रिय: ।। (VI-1) ।।

Lord says "O Arjun a person who is doing his duties in the life and at the same time remains unattached to the worldly attractions is the real Yogi or a pious man. But on the other hand who is doing Yajnas etc. but at the same time influenced by the worldly attractions and have negative tendencies of lust, anger, greed, attachment, ego, pride and hatred, cannot reach God. He cannot be called a Yogi."

यं संन्यासमिति प्राहुर्योगं तं विद्धि पाण्डव ।
न ह्यसंन्यस्तसंकल्पो योगी भवति कश्चन ।। (VI-2) ।।

"The renunciation of the worldly attractions is very necessary to become a Yogi, without leaving them it is not possible to become a Yogi. The negative tendencies must be renounced to become a Yogi in the actual sense."

आरूरूक्षोर्मुनेर्योगं कर्म कारणमुच्यते ।
योगारूढस्य तस्यैव शम: कारणमुच्यते ।। (VI-3) ।।

"A person who does not harm anyone, not desire anything from any person, does not have any ill will towards others, discharges his worldly duties away from the negative tendencies is the real Karma Yogi. He does not have any attachments in life. He lives in the world at the same time is not attracted by the allurements, is Yogi in the complete sense."

A Yogi has to sacrifice many things in his life. It is very difficult and hard path. But a person who is determined finds no difficulty. When a person leaves all the desires behind, he attains the state of a Yogi. All other desires become secondary to him, he absorbes himself in the pursuit of truth and knowledge.

यदा हि नेन्द्रियार्थेषु न कर्मस्वनुषज्जते ।
सर्वसंकल्पसन्यासी योगारूढस्तदोच्यते ।। (VI-4) ।।

"O Arjun, so a person at any stage becomes indifferent to the negative forces of lust, anger, greed, attachment, ego, hatred etc. becomes a Yogi. All the attachments of the world do not effect him at this stage."

उद्धरेदात्मनात्मानं नात्मानमवसादयेत् ।

आत्मैव ह्यत्मनो बन्धुरात्मैव रिपुरात्मनः ।। (VI-5) ।।

बन्धुरात्मात्मनस्तस्य येनात्मैवात्मना जितः ।

अनात्मनस्तु शत्रुत्वे वर्तेतात्मैव शत्रुवत ।। (VI-6) ।।

"A person should try to free himself from the vices in this world. He is his own friend and at the same time enemy too. One, who moves on the right path can really enjoy the stay in this world. A person who is able to achieve this finds himself in complete happiness and in perfect state of mind on the other hand who is absorbed in the vices finds himself bound by the difficulties. He is like a person who has darkness all around and is unable to come out the cycle of births and deaths."

जितात्मनः प्रशान्तस्य परमात्मा समाहितः ।

शीतोष्णसुखदुःखेषु तथा मानापमानयोः ।। (VI-7) ।।

ज्ञानविज्ञान तृप्तात्मा कूटस्थो विजितेन्द्रियः ।

युक्त इत्युच्यते योगी समलोष्टाश्मकाच्चनः ।। (VI-8) ।।

"By attaining perfection the person is free from all bondages of life. He is equally balanced whether it is happiness or otherwise. He is termed as a Yukta Yogi or a complete Yogi. Comforts and discomforts become immaterial to him. By positive deeds he becomes complete and perfect. He leaves the world at a positive note and with contentment."

सुहृन्मित्रार्युदासीनमध्यस्थद्वेष्यबन्धुषु ।

साधुष्वपि च पापेषु समबुद्धिर्विशिष्यते ।। (VI-9) ।।

योगी युंज्जीत सततमात्मानं रहसि स्थितः ।

एकाकी यतचित्तात्मा निराशीरपरिग्रहः ।। (VI-10) ।।

"A person who is pious and perfect is equidistanced from friends or enemies. He does not have any ill feelings towards anyone, and is helpful in nature. He does not harm anybody. He is helpful and positive in his approach both towards friends as well as foes.

A Yogi is always in a state of calm. His time is spent in meditation and in the service of mankind. His approach to life is positive, constructive and helpful to all the mankind. He does not desire anything and accepts whatever comes to him as the gift of God. He remains calm and steady in difficulties and faces them with determination and challenge."

शुचौ देशे प्रतिष्टाप्य स्थिरमासनमात्मनः ।

नात्युच्छ्रितं नातिनीचं चैलाजिन कुशोत्तरम ।। (VI-11) ।।

"A Yogi should meditate in a noiseless surroundings. The surrounding should be calm and peaceful, near the nature. A Yogi should sit on a mat and do the meditation."

तत्रैकांग्र मनः कृत्वा यतचित्तेन्द्रियक्रियः ।

उपविश्यासने युज्याद्योगमात्मविशुद्धये ।। (VI-12) ।।

समं कायशिरोग्रींव धारयन्नचलं स्थिरः ।

सम्प्रेक्ष्य नासिकाग्रं स्वं दिशश्चानवलोकयन् ।। (VI-13) ।।

"Sitting on a mat, the Yogi should concentrate on an object. He should be in a state of calm without any disturbance. The Yogi should not think of any other thing at the time of doing meditation. It is difficult in the initial stage but with practice can be achieved."

प्रशान्तात्मा विगतभीर्ब्रह्मचारिव्रते स्थितः ।

मनः संयम्य मच्चित्तो युक्त आसीत मत्परः ।। (VI-14) ।।

युजन्नैवं सदात्मानं योगी नियतमानसः ।

शान्तिं निर्वाणपरमां मत्संस्थामधिगच्छति ॥ (VI-15) ॥

The Lord is explaining to Arjun about meditation and the correct way to perform the same. He says "A person should sit straight on a mat, fixing his sight and thoughts in God. While doing meditation the person should select a fix time and a fix place for doing the same. He should not change places and practice celibacy during that period. He will definitely reach Me (God) in course of time and attain salvation or Mokshya.

नात्यश्नतस्तु योगोऽस्ति न चैकान्तमनश्नतः ।

न चातिस्वप्नशीलस्य जाग्रतो नैव चार्जुन ॥ (VI-16) ॥

युक्ताहारविहारस्य युक्तचेष्टस्य कर्मसु ।

युक्तास्वप्नावबोधस्य योगो भवति दुःखहा ॥ (VI-17) ॥

Krishna says "O Arjun the excess of everything is bad. We must discipline our life. Too much of eating is also harmful. Having food twice a day is sufficient for the body. Similarly too much of sleeping is also harmful. Sleeping during the day should be avoided and will not give sound sleep at night. At the same time taking less food or sleep is also harmful. A person must balance his habits as too much or too little of anything is bad and harmful."

Moderation is the keyword in the above two verses. In short, the Lord advises that a devotee should live a moderate life following the control path and avoiding the extremes to achieve peace and satisfaction in life.

यदा विनियतं चित्तमात्मन्येवावतिष्ठते ।

निःस्पृहः सर्वकामेभ्यो युक्त इत्युच्यते तदा ॥ (VI-18) ॥

यथा दीपो निवातस्थो नेंगते सोपमा स्मृता ।

योगिनो यतचित्तस्य युञ्जतो योगमात्मनः ॥ (VI-19) ॥

"With the disciplined life the devotee elevates himself and thus become a Yogi. In a calm atmosphere where there is no disturbance a flame keeps on burning smoothly and steadily, in the sameway the life of such devotee becomes calm, quiet and perfect. He has no worries, he is devoid of expectations, has no enmity with anyone. In other words he is a pious and loveable human being. He becomes a true Yogi."

यत्रोपरमते चित्तं निरूद्धं योगसेवया ।
यत्र चैवात्मनात्मानं पश्यन्नात्मनि तुष्यति ॥ (VI-20) ॥
सुखमात्यन्तिकं यत्तद्बुद्धिग्राह्यमतीन्द्रियम ।
वेत्ति यत्र न चैवायं स्थितश्चलति तत्त्वत: ॥ (VI-21) ॥

"With regular practice a person becomes a Yogi or learned one. He is calm and in a state of fulfillment. He attains happiness and tranquility. No other attachments can influence him anymore. He finds himself in a state of calm, serene and happy frame of mind. All the other allurements of life become secondary to him."

Lord Krishna is explaining, Arjun, regarding the practice of Yoga in life. A person gets peace of mind and stability in life and the God blesses him with contentment and happiness.

यं लब्ध्वा चापरं लाभं मन्यते नाधिकं तत: ।
यस्मिन्स्थितो न दु:खेन गुरूणापि विचाल्यते ॥ (VI-22) ॥
तं विद्याद्दु:खसंयोगवियोगं योगसंज्ञितम् ।
स निश्चयेन योक्तव्यो योगोऽनिर्विण्णचेतसा ॥ (VI-23) ॥

"With the knowledge thus gained a devotee finds himself near God. All other things become of no consequence to him. Even in misfortunes he remains calm and is not disturbed in mind and heart. His mission on this earth is achieved and he keeps himself preoccupied with the positive activities and helping the mankind.

संकल्पप्रभवान्कांमास्त्यकत्वा सर्वानिशेषत: ।
मनसैवेन्द्रियग्रामं विनियम्य समन्तत: ॥ (VI-24) ॥
शनै: शनैरूपरमेद्बुद्धया धृतिगृहीतया ।
आत्मसंस्थं मन: कृत्वा न किंचिदपि चिन्तयेत् ॥ (VI-25) ॥

यतो यतो निश्चरति मनंश्चंचलमस्थिरम् ।
ततस्ततो नियम्यैतदात्मन्येव वशं नयेत् ।। (VI-26) ।।

"The mind wonders in the worldly objects and attractions. A Yogi should desist from them and concentrate on the object while meditating. The mind after sometime becomes calm and the devotee is able to perform the meditation without any disturbance. Slowly but surely he is able to achieve full control on the senses and his mind becomes calm. At this stage the person finds himself at peace, the worldly attractions do not effect him anymore."

प्रशान्तमनसं ह्येनं योगिनं सुखमुत्तमम ।
उपैति शांतरजसं ब्रह्मभूतमकल्मषम् ।। (VI-27) ।।
सुज्जन्नैवं सदात्मानं योगी विगतकल्मषः ।
सुखेन ब्रह्मसंस्पर्शमत्यन्तं सुखमश्नुते ।। (VI-28) ।।

"A person (devotee) attains happiness and his deeds (Karmas) lead him to Mokshya *i.e.*, salvation. Happiness and unhappiness become immaterial to him. He finds himself near the Almighty. His thoughts are pure and he attains real happiness and contentment in his life."

सर्वभूतस्थमात्मानं सर्वभूतानि चात्मनि ।
ईक्षते योगयुक्तात्मा सर्वत्र समदर्शनः ।। (VI-29) ।।
यो मां पश्यति सर्वत्र सर्वं च मयि पश्यति ।
तस्यांह न प्रणश्यामि स च मे न प्रणश्यति ।। (VI-30) ।।

"A Yogi thus becomes a part of God. All his actions and activities are in pursuit of the truth. The Jeevatma and the Parmatma become one. He feels my (God) soul in the whole mankind and everywhere he finds the presence of God."

सर्वभूतस्थितं यो मां भजत्येकत्वमास्थितः ।
सर्वथा वर्तमानोऽपि स योगी मयि वर्तते ।। (VI-31) ।।
आत्मौपम्येन सर्वत्र समं पश्यति योऽर्जुन ।
सुखं वा यदि वा दुःखं स योगी परमोमतः ।। (VI-32) ।।

"O Arjun the Yogi sees my soul in all the creatures. For him the woes and sorrows of others become his, and he tries to alleviate their sorrows with his pious deeds."

The main idea of the above few verses is almost the same *i.e.*, they tell us about the qualities of a Yogi (holy man). He lives in this world for helping the mankind in distress.

योऽयं योगस्त्वया प्रोक्तः साम्येन मधुसूदन ।
एतस्यांह न पश्यामि चंचलत्वात्स्थितिं स्थिराम् ।। (VI-33) ।।

Arjun says "O Krishna what you have described about Yogi, I feel that I do not have any such qualities. I am not in a position to achieve that because I do not have these qualities ought to be in a Yogi. The mind is very fickle and I do not think I will be able to achieve it."

चंचलं हि मनः कृष्ण प्रमाथि बलवद्दृष्ढम् ।
तस्यांह निग्रंह मन्ये वायोरिव सुदुष्करम् ।। (VI-34) ।।

"O Krishna my mind is very restless and it is very difficult to have control over the same. It is just like wind. As it is difficult to have control over it. If a person cannot have control over mind he cannot become Yogi. How can I become the same? Please enlighten me."

Arjun is disturbed and he requests Lord Krishna to guide him.

असंशयं महाबाहो मनो दुर्निगहं चलम् ।
अभ्यासेन तु कौन्तेय वैराग्येण च गृह्यते ।। (VI-35) ।।

Shri Krishna consoles Arjun "You should not be worried about the mind. It is true that it is very difficult to tame mind. But with regular practice it can be achieved. You should also have a sense of detachment in you. So with these two traits you will be able to have full control on your mind."

असंयतात्मना योगो दुष्प्राप इति में मतिः ।
वश्यात्मना तु यतता शक्योऽवाप्तुमुपायतः ।। (VI-36) ।।

"If the mind is not under control a devotee cannot perfect the art of Yoga. When you are able to do this, at that stage you will be able to perfect Yoga as well."

It is very important to have control over the mind and the body. Therefore a person who is unable to control his mind and body it is very difficult for him to practice Yoga. But with regular practice and with a sense of detachment a person can achieve the same. The advantage of Yoga is that the evil tendencies are under control and mind and body become pure.

अयतिः श्रद्धयोपेतो योगाच्चलितमानसः ।
अप्राप्य योगसंसिद्धिं कां गतिं कृष्ण गच्छति ।। (VI-37) ।।
कच्चिन्नोभयविभ्रष्टश्छिन्नाभ्रमिव नश्यति ।
अप्रतिष्ठो महाबाहो विमूढो ब्रह्मणः पथि ।। (VI-38) ।।
एतन्मे संशय कृष्ण छेत्तुमर्हस्यशेषतः ।
त्वदन्यः संशयस्यास्य छेत्ता नह्युपपद्यते ।। (VI-39) ।।

Arjun is doubtful and asks Krishna "O Lord if a devotee is unable to have control on his mind and body, will it have any effect on Yoga or meditation. It is very difficult to have control on mind and body. Does the meditation comes to an end? Will he be able to get the knowledge of Yoga at all? I am unable to come to any definite conclusion. O Lord as you have full authority on Yoga, please let me know the results, when a devotee is unable to control his mind and body."

पार्थ नैवेह नामुत्र विनाशस्तस्य विद्यते ।
नहि कल्याणकृत्कश्चिद्दुर्गतिं तात गच्छति ।। (VI-40) ।।

"O Parth (Arjun) a person who has started moving on this path I (God) do not forget him even he might have not completed the full journey and had left it in between due to any reason. I always remain with him too."

That shows the benevolence of Almighty. Even if a person remembers Him for a smaller period even then the God stands by him at the time of difficulty and need.

प्राप्य पुण्यकृतांल्लोकानुषित्वा शाश्वतीः समाः ।
शुचीनां श्रीमतां गेहे योगभ्रष्टोऽभिजायते ।। (VI-41) ।।

"O Arjun even this devotee of mine reaches Me (God) and goes to heaven because of his pious deeds. He stays there for some time and is born again in a wealthy and godly family to complete the balance of his Yoga."

अथवा योगिनामेव कुले भवति धीमताम् ।
एतद्धि दुर्लभतरं लोके जन्म यदीदृशम् ।। (VI-42) ।।

"When this devotee comes to the world again, he picks up where he had left earlier and restart the Yoga once again. But such type of examples are rare. This time he completes the same and rests in heaven after the work has been completed."

तत्र तं बुद्धिसंयोगं लभते पौर्वदेहिकम् ।
यतते च ततो भूयः संसिद्धौ कुरूनन्दन ।। (VI-43) ।।
पूर्वाभ्यासेन तेनैव ह्रियते ह्यवशोऽपि सः ।
जिज्ञासुरपि योगस्य शब्दब्रह्मातिवर्तते ।। (VI-44) ।।

Krishna further explains to Arjun and says "The devotee who had lost the Yoga half way or could not complete it, this time he works hard and reaches his goal *i.e.*, attaining the Supreme power. He takes birth in a wealthy family and enjoys the world at the same time remain busy in the spiritual work."

प्रयत्नाद्यतमानस्तु योगी संशुद्धकिल्बिषः ।
अनेक जन्मसंसिद्धस्ततो याति परां गतिम् ।। (VI-45) ।।
तपस्विभ्योऽधिको योगी ज्ञानिभ्योऽपि मतोऽधिकः ।
कर्मभ्यश्चाधिको योगी तस्माद्योगी भवार्जुन ।। (VI-46) ।।

"Thus with regular practice and hard work a devotee attains perfection and becomes a Yogi. This is the highest state that a devotee reaches. He is much above even scholars of spiritual knowledge. So O Arjun I (Krishna) want you to become a Yogi."

योगिनामपि सर्वेषां मद्गतेनान्तरात्मना ।
श्रद्धावान्भजते यो मां स मे युक्ततमो मतः ।। (VI-47) ।।

"O Arjun the devotee of mine keeps on doing meditation and performing his duties in this world in a positive way, ultimately reaches Me (God). He is able to free himself from all the bondages of life, negative tendencies and unite with the power supreme. With hard work and sincere efforts he attains complete peace of mind and reaches his destination *i.e.*, heaven."

CHAPTER VII

In this chapter Krishna is Explaining to Arjun about the Divine Knowledge and How to Gain the Same

मय्यासक्तमनाः पार्थ योगं युंजन्मदाश्रयः ।
अंसशयं समग्रं मां यथा ज्ञास्यसि तच्छृणु ।। (VII-1) ।।

Lord Krishna says "O Parth (Arjun) listen to me. I love a devotee who comes to me for protection and salvation (Mokshya). A person who comes to me with devotion and faith I rescue him from all the difficulties and sins. I take him in my protection."

We love our children, relations and friends but when the same love and affection is projected towards God, it becomes devotion or Bhakti. So when a person starts remembering God it become devotion or Bhakti *i.e.*, the higher form of love. When a person remembers God with full faith the Lord does respond to the devotee and the person becomes a Yogi.

ज्ञानं तेऽहं सविज्ञानमिंदं वक्ष्याम्यशेषतः ।
यज्ज्ञात्वा नेह भूयोऽन्यज्ज्ञातव्यमवशिष्यते ।। (VII-2) ।।

"O Arjun I will now reveal to you the secret of full knowledge. After gaining this you will not need anything more because it is complete in itself. With this knowledge you will be able to see with clear mind as to what is right for you. You will have a clear vision as to fight or not after gaining this knowledge."

मनुष्याणां सहस्रेषु कश्चिद्यतति सिद्धये ।
यततामपि सिद्धानां कश्चिन्मां वेत्ति तत्त्वतः ।। (VII-3) ।।

"O Arjun from thousands of persons a few reach Me (God) and from those thousands hardly one or two can understand Me and are able to reach Me."

In other words the Lord explains to Arjun that a very few devotees ultimately reach the final stage. Many leave half way and only those can reach the destination who are steadfast and have a strong will. It is just like a long race, many start but a few reach the post or destination, majority of them leave in between and are unable to reach the finishing point. The same way thousands of people worship god but a few reach him finally. It is same as many people start climbing a maintain but a few reach the peak. But those who have faith and determination attain Him and salvation.

भूमिरापोऽनलो वायुः खं मनो बुद्धिरेव च ।

अहंकार इतीयं मे भिन्ना प्रकृतिरष्टधा ।। (VII-4) ।।

अपरेयमितस्त्वन्यां प्रकृतिं विद्धि मे पराम् ।

जीवभूतां महाबाहो ययेद धार्यते जगत् ।। (VII-5) ।।

Lord Krishna says "O Arjun my nature consists of two parts *i.e.*, Jeeva and Pribriti. The Jeeva forms the upper *i.e.*, the universe and the lower consists of earth, water, fire, air sky, mind, intellect and ego."

These natures can be compared with an ocean. While the upper layer is very violent and stormy, at the same time the lower is very calm and quite. The Lord tells Arjun that God is the creature of all these natures and the master of the same.

एतद्योनीनि भूतानि सर्वाणीत्युपधारय ।

अहं कृत्स्नस्य जगतः प्रभवः प्रलयस्तथा ।। (VII-6) ।।

"I am the creator and destroyer of the universe. All are born out of Me (God) and ultimately submerge in Me in the final."

The Lord is explaining to Arjun that god is very powerful and He only controls this universe, therefore he (Arjun) should not worry anymore regarding the outcome of the coming battle, as God is the creator as well destroyer of this world. As such he should not worry at all of the consequences of this war with Kaurvas.

मत्तः परतरं नान्यत्किंचिदस्ति धनंजय ।

मयि सर्वमिंद प्रोतं सूत्रे मणिगणा इव ।। (VII-7) ।।

Krishna says "O Dhananjaya (Arjun) I (God) am like a thread in a garland. A garland have so many flowers, they are all bound together by the string (thread). Similarly all the mankind is just like flowers bound together by the force of God and get strength from the power supreme."

रसोऽहमप्सु कौन्तेय प्रभास्मि शशिसूर्ययोः ।

प्रणवः सर्ववेदेषु शब्दः खे पौरूषं नृषु ॥ (VII-8) ॥

पुण्यो गन्धः पृथिव्यां च तेजश्चास्मि विभावसौ ।

जीवनं सर्वभूतेषु तपश्चास्मि तपस्विषु ॥ (VII-9) ॥

"O Kaunteya (Arjun) I (God) am the taste in water, the light in the sun and moon is due to Me. I am the force behind them. I am present in flowers as fragrance. I am the pessance in Yogis and sages. I am the supporting system in all the creations."

The Lord is explaining to Arjun that the Almighty God is the force behind everything in the universe.

बीजं मां सर्वभूतानां विद्धि पार्थं सनातनम् ।

बुद्धिर्बुद्धिमतामस्मि तेजस्तेजस्विनामहम् ॥ (VII-10) ॥

बलं वलवतार्मास्म कामरागविवर्जितम् ।

धर्माविरूद्धो भूतेषु कामोऽस्मि भरतर्षभ ॥ (VII-11) ॥

"O Parth (Arjun), I am the seed in fruits. I am the intelligence of the learned people. I am the strength of the brave."

Lord Krishna is explaining to Arjun that the presence of God is everywhere in the world. In other words Krishna tells Arjun that the actual and main force behind all is the strength of God.

ये चैव सात्विका भावा राजसास्तामसाश्च ये ।

मत्त एवेति तान्विद्धि न त्वहं तेषु ते मयि ॥ (VII-12) ॥

"O Arjun the thoughts of nobility, Karma and evil are put by me in the individual. I give all these tendencies to a person, but it depends upon him to choose from them. All the good and evil persons are in my body, but I am not with all the persons *i.e.*, I am not with the evil forces. I remain with true and noble person. Therefore it is the noble person who finds myself near him and not the evil minded person."

त्रिभिर्गुणमयैर्भावैरेभिः सर्वमिदं जगत्।

मोहितं नाभिजानाति मामेभ्यः परमव्ययम् ॥ (VII-13) ॥

दैवी ह्येषा गुणमयी मम माया दुरत्यया ।

मामेव ये प्रपद्यन्ते मायामेतां तरन्ति ते ॥ (VII-14) ॥

"There are three types of persons in this world. Noble (Satvic), Karma (Rajasic) and Evil (Tamasic). Due to my Yogmaya (illusion) they are all busy in their daily routines. But the one who turns towards Me (God) I help him in every possible way. It is only the pious and noble people who try to search Me. So O Arjun what you are watching all around, it is all due to my Yogmaya."

न मां दुष्कृतिनो मूढाः पापद्यन्ते नराधमाः ।

माययापहृतज्ञाना आसुरं भावमाश्रिताः ॥ (VII-15) ॥

"Those who do not entrust Me (God) are not wise, they do not understand about the positive aspect of life. They are allured by the attachments of this world as such are ill informed and full of negative tendencies. But those who come to me I help them in every possible way and bless them with complete peace of mind, fulfillment and happiness."

चतुर्विधा भजन्ते मां जनाः सुकृतिनोऽर्जुन ।

आर्तो जिज्ञासुरर्थार्थी ज्ञानी च भरतर्षभ ॥ (VII-16) ॥

तेषां ज्ञानी नित्ययुक्त एकभक्तिर्विशिष्यते ।

प्रियो हि ज्ञानिनोऽत्यर्थमहं स च मम प्रियः ॥ (VII-17) ॥

Lord Krishna says "O Arjun there are four types of devotees who worship Me (God). The first are those who worship me for the material gains. They desire something and come to me so that I may grant that wish. The second type are those who are in some difficulty. They come to me with a request to take them out of that difficulty. The third type are those who are in search of truth and lastly are those who do not expect anything in return. They do not ask for any help or favour out of Me. O Arjun I love the last type of my devotees. They do not wish anything and come to me with love and affection. I also love them and give my affection."

उदाराः सर्व एवैते ज्ञानी त्वात्मैव मे मतम् ।

आस्थितः स हि युक्तात्मा मामेवानुत्तमां गतिम् ॥ (VII-18) ॥

"I like all these four type of my devotees. But still I have a special regard for the last type who ultimately become my part."

बहूनां जन्मनामन्ते ज्ञानवान्मां प्रपद्यते ।

वासुदेवः सर्वमिति स महात्मा सुदुर्लभा ॥ (VII-19) ॥

"Such devotees of mine are very rare or in a microscopic minority. They are Yogis or sages and merge with Me in the final."

The Lord is explaining to Arjun that the worship done without any expectations is of the highest order. They are many times higher than the other devotees and closest to the Almighty *i.e.*, God. So we should worship without any expectation and returns. This worship is of the highest order and the best.

कामैस्तैस्तै र्हृत ज्ञानाः प्रपद्यन्तेऽन्यदेवताः ।

तं तं नियममास्थाय प्रकृत्या नियताः स्वया ॥ (VII-20) ॥

यो यो यां यां तनुं भक्तः श्रद्धया र्चितु मिच्छति।

तस्य तस्याचलां श्रद्धां तामेव विदधाम्यहम् ॥ (VII-21) ॥

स तया श्रद्धया युक्तस्तस्यांरा धनमोहते ।

लभते च ततः कामान्मयैव विहितान्हि तान् ॥ (VII-22) ॥

Krishna says "O Arjun I even help these persons who do not come to Me but worship lesser Gods. I do not mind such persons because ultimately they come to me in the final."

By these remarks we can understand that in that period also other religions or faiths must have been there besides Arya Dharma. The other faiths (religions) as it seems might be the older civilizations *i.e.*, Roman, Egyptian. Babilonian, Chinese or Greek etc. So it appears that the Lord might have pointed to these civilizations as the other faiths. He says to Arjun that whatever any one worships ultimately comes to Me (God). It shows that the Lord had no ill will towards others faiths too.

अन्तवत्तु फलं तेषां तभ्दवत्यल्पमेधसाम् ।

देवान्देवयजो यान्ति मद्‌भक्ता यान्ति मामपि ।। (VII-23) ।।

अव्यक्तं व्यक्तिमापन्नं मन्यन्ते मामबुद्धयः ।

परं भावमजानन्तो ममाव्ययमनुत्तमम् ।। (VII-24) ।।

"Those who love and understand Me come in my fold and attain perfection. But those who worship lesser Gods go to them and their journey is longer. The persons who consider Me as human being are wrong in their assessments, because I am eternal, neither I die and nor born, I am present in the universe all the time and it is happening from the time immemorial and will go on happening in the same way in future as well. I belong to the entire universe and am immortal."

नाहं प्रकाशः सर्वस्य योगमायासमावृतः ।

मूढोऽयं नाभिजानाति लोको मामजमव्ययम् ।। (VII-25) ।।

वेदाहं समतीतानि वर्तमानानि चार्जुन ।

भविष्याणि च भूतानि मां तु वेद न कश्चन ।। (VII-26) ।।

"O Arjun who are ill informed they do not know that I (God) am immortal with my Maya (illusion) I keep my secrets and only those persons can understand Me who have love, affection and faith in Me. I know all the people who have come on this earth, are present and those who will come here in future. I have complete knowledge about all the mankind, because I am the driving force behind all the actions."

The Lord says that only those people can recognize him who are pure at heart have faith in him and an urge to unite with the Almighty. Therefore faith and devotion are required to reach or attain salvation and peace of mind.

इच्छाद्वेषसमुत्थेन द्वन्द्वमोहेन भारत ।

सर्वभूतानि संमोहं सर्गे यान्ति परंतप ॥ (VII-27) ॥

येषां त्वन्तगतं पापं जनानां पुण्यकर्मणाम् ।

ते द्वन्द्वमोहनिर्मुक्ता भजन्ते मां दृढ़व्रताः ॥ (VII-28) ॥

"O Arjun those persons who have lack of spiritual knowledge, they are unable to understand and recognise Me. They are engulfed by the negative tendencies *i.e.*, lust, anger, greed, attachment, ego, hate and jealousy as such keep on taking birth after birth and do not get salvation or Mokshya and are unable to come out of the clutches of these evil tendencies. Only those persons reach me who have destroyed these evil forces. They become pure as such are able to attain Me."

जरामरणमोक्षाय ममाश्रित्य यतन्ति ये ।

ते ब्रह्म तद्विदुः कृत्स्नमध्यात्मं कर्म चाखिलम् ॥ (VII-29) ॥

साधिभूताधिदैवं मां साधियज्ञं च ये विदुः ।

प्रयाणकालेऽपि च मां ते विदुर्युक्तचेतसः ॥ (VII-30) ॥

"The persons who thus gain knowledge and faith in Me (God) ultimately unite with Me. The persons who have banished the evil tendencies of lust anger, greed, attachments, ego, hatred and jealousy etc. become calm and pious.

They know that God is present in all objects in different forms. Such devotees of mine attain salvation or Mokshya and reach Me (God) in the end.

A devotee should have faith, urge and confidence to attain the Almighty. The persons who are able to do this, they are able to reach the final destination *i.e.* God.

CHAPTER VIII

Arjun is not Clear in His Mind Regarding Brahma (The Creator), and Karma (Spiritualism). He is Requesting Krishna to Explain to Him the Same in a Very Simple Language

किं तद्ब्रह्म किमध्यात्मं किं कर्म पुरूषोत्तम ।
अधिभूतं च किं प्रोक्तमधिदैवं किमुच्येत ॥ (VIII-1) ॥
अधियज्ञः कथं कोऽत्र देहेऽस्मिन्मधुसूदन ।
प्रयाणकाले च कथं ज्ञेयोऽसि नियतात्मभिः ॥ (VIII-2) ॥

O Krishna says Arjun "I am still not clear in my mind about Brahma (God) and Karma (spiritualism). Will you please explain to me in a simple language the meaning of the two?"

Arjun has confusion in his mind about the things Krishna told him in the previous chapter. So he once again requests him to explain to him about God and Karma or spiritualism.

अक्षंर ब्रह्म परमं स्वभावोऽध्यात्ममुच्यते ।
भूतभावोभ्दवकरो विसर्गः कर्मसंज्ञितः ॥ (VIII-3) ॥
अधिभूतं क्षरो भावः पुरूषश्चाधिदैवतम् ।
अधियज्ञोऽहमेवात्र देहे देहभृंता वर ॥ (VIII-4) ॥

Krishna says to Arjun "O Parth (Arjun) you should know about the two things clearly. Brahma is the ultimate force *i.e.*, God. He is the creator of this universe. Karma *i.e.*, spiritualism is the source of soul. Those who discard tendencies of lust, anger, greed, attachements, ego, hatred and jealousy become calm and pious. They know, as water is present in many shapes *i.e.*, vapours, snow, clouds, rivers etc. similarly God is present in all the objects in different forms. So such devotees of mine attain salvation or Mokshya and reach Me in the end."

A devotee should have faith, urge and confidence to attain the Almighty. The persons who are able to do this, they are able to reach the final destination *i.e.*, God. Through Karma a person is able to get rid of his evil tendencies *i.e.*, lust, anger, greed, attachments, ego, hatred and jealousy. By doing Karma a person is in a position to discard these evil forces and attain Mokshya or salvation. After getting control over these tendencies the person becomes pure and thus is able to reach God."

अन्तकाले च मामेव स्मरन्मुक्त्वा कलेवरम् ।
यः प्रयाति स मभ्दावं याति नास्त्यत्र संशयः ।। (VIII-5) ।।
यं यं वापि स्मरन्भांव त्यजत्यन्ते कलेवरम् ।
तं तमेवैति कौन्तेय सदा तभ्दावभावितः ।। (VIII-6) ।।
तस्मात्सर्वेषु कालेषु मामनुस्मर युध्य च ।
मय्यर्पितमनाबुद्धिर्मामेवैष्यस्य संशयम् ।। (VIII-7) ।।

Krishna says "O Kaunteya (Son of Kunti) at the time of death whatever your thought process is, that is embedded in you. Those thoughts have a very lasting impression and are carried in the next birth. The person who thinks about Me (God) naturally comes to Me. He has not to undergo the cycle of rebirths. Therefore O Parth put all your thoughts towards Me (God) and get ready for the battle, because who dies performing his duties gets Mokshya or salvation."

Here again Krishna is reassuring Arjun that his duty is to fight and if he dies doing his duty in the battle field he will definitely go to heaven. This equally applies to mankind in general. If one keeps on doing his duties truthfully in the battlefield of life remembering God, he will definitely be blessed by God and unite with Him after completing his journey on this earth.

अभ्यासयोग युक्तेन चेतसा नान्यगामिना ।
परमं पुरूषं दिव्य याति पार्थानुचिन्तयन् ।। (VIII-8) ।।
कविं पुराणं अनुशासितामणोरणीयांस मनु स्मरेद्यः ।
सर्वस्य धातारमचिन्त्यरूपमादित्यवर्णं तमसः परस्तात ।। (VIII-9) ।।

Krishna says "O Parth (Arjun) a devotee who remembers me with dedication I see that he comes to me ultimately. He knows that God is most powerful, present everywhere in this universe. This type of Yogi is close to my heart and I (God) protect him from all the evil forces."

प्रयाणकाले मनसाचलेन भक्त्यायुक्तो योगबलेन चैव ।
भ्रुवोर्मध्ये प्राणमावेश्य सम्यक् सतं परं पुरूषमुपैति दिव्यम् ।। (VIII-10) ।।

"O Arjun at the time of death if a devotee centres his soul in between the two eyes on the forehead and remembers God is sure to get Mokshya or salvation. He goes to the abode of Almighty."

यदक्षरं वेदविदो वदन्ति विशंति यद्यतयो वीतरागाः ।
यदिच्छन्तो ब्रह्मचर्यं चरन्ति तत्ते पदं संग्रहेण प्रवक्ष्ये ।। (VIII-11) ।।
सर्वद्वाराणि संयम्य मनो हृदि निरूध्य च ।
मूध्न्यार्धायात्मनः प्राणमा स्थितो योगधारणाम् ।। (VIII-12) ।।

"O Arjun there are saints and sages who reach the extreme stage of Yoga by practising complete celibacy. I will tell you about this. These saints practice by blocking their sensory organs from the outside world by focusing their soul in between the forehead. By this Yoga they reach the ultimate goal of devotion and Bhakti towards God."

This is very difficult Yogic exercise and only those saints can attain it who have practised it for a long time. Though this type of sadhna (worship) is extreme difficult but still we can come across these kind of saints and sages in this world. Through faith and confidence a person can achieve anything in his life. So there is nothing difficult to achieve with regular practice.

ओमित्येकांक्षर ब्रह्म व्याहरन्मामनुस्मरन् ।
यः प्रयाति त्यजन्देहं स याति परमां गतिम् ।। (VIII-13) ।।

"At the time of death if a person recites the word "Brahm" it is very auspicious and divine. That devotee of mine reaches the Almighty in heaven, and gets freedom from the cycle of births and deaths."

अनन्यचेताः सततं यो मां स्मरति नित्यशः ।
तस्यांह सुलभः पार्थ नित्ययुक्तस्य योगिनः ।। (VIII-14) ।।

Krishna says to Arjun "O Parth the devotee who remembers Me with faith and trust I (God) am always near him at all times and free him from all obstacles."

मामुपेत्य पुनर्जन्म दुःखालयमशाश्वतम् ।
नाप्नुवन्ति महात्मानः संसिद्धिं परमां गताः ।। (VIII-15) ।।

"The devotee who can focus his thoughts to God no doubt reaches Him. Such a Yogi (Pious soul) attains perfection and there is nothing left for him to attain more. He comes out of the cycle of births and deaths and attains God."

आब्रह्म भुवनाल्लोकाः पुनरावर्तिनोऽर्जुन ।
मामुपेत्य तु कौन्तेय पुनर्जन्म न विद्यते ।। (VIII-16) ।।

Krishna says "O Kaunteya (Son of Kunti, Arjun) a devotee who comes to Me (God) I grant him final salvation or Mokshya. He comes out of the cycle of births and deaths. I grant him total peace of mind and happiness."

The Lord ensures Arjun that any one who remembers God with faith and devotion, the God definitely comes to his rescue at the time of need. Only, the devotee should have faith and self confidence. The god protects the pious and true followers in need and there should be no doubt regarding the same.

सहस्त्रयुगपर्यन्तमहर्यद् ब्रह्मणो विदुः ।
रात्रि युगसहस्त्रान्तां तेऽहोरात्र विदो जनाः ।। (VIII-17) ।।

"O Arjun a Yogi (scholar) knows that one day of Brahma is equivalent to one thousand times of the four Yugas and also one night of the same is equal to one thousand times of the same.

In other words the day or night of Brahma is infinity *i.e.*, we cannot even calculate the same.

अव्यक्ताद्व्यक्तयः सर्वाः प्रभवन्त्यहरागमे ।
रात्र्यागमे प्रलीयन्ते तत्रैवाव्यक्तसंज्ञके ।। (VIII-18) ।।

"O Arjun the learned person (scholar of Vedas) knows that Brahma has created this universe out of him at the time of day and destroys the same at the time of night."

भूतग्राम: स एवायं भूत्वा भूत्वा प्रलीयते ।
रात्र्यागमेऽवश: पार्थ प्रभवत्यहरागमे ॥ (VIII-19) ॥

"O Parth Brahma has created all the living and non-living (universal) objects. They all go the chosen paths and when the night of Brahma falls they all are destroyed or go away from this universe. This process keeps on repeating from the time immemorial."

परस्तस्मात्तु भावोऽन्योऽव्यक्तोऽव्यक्तात्सनातन: ।
य: स सर्वेषु भूतेषु नश्यत्सु न विनश्यति ॥ (VIII-20) ॥

"O Arjun even with this cycle of destruction and revival by Brahma, there is one thing which never dies *i.e.*, spirit or our soul. This is indestructible and lives throughout."

अव्यक्तोऽक्षर इत्युक्तस्तमाहु: परमां गतिम् ।
यं प्राप्य न निवर्तन्ते तद्धाम परमं मम ॥ (VIII-21) ॥

"The soul never dies, and keeps on coming on this earth again and again in new forms. The actual home of the soul is Akshara which is My (God) abode. The devotee who reaches this with his efforts and faith come to my abode. He gets freedom or Mokshya and comes out the regular cycle of births and deaths."

पुरूष: स पर: पार्थ भक्त्या लभ्यस्त्वनन्यया ।
यस्यान्त: स्थानि भूतानि येन सर्वमिंद ततम् ॥ (VIII-22) ॥
यत्र काले त्वनावृत्तिमावृत्तिं चैव योगिन: ।
प्रयाता यान्ति तं कालं वक्ष्यामि भरतर्षभ ॥ (VIII-23) ॥

"O Arjun the supreme is that who can give help to a person who comes to him for protection. O Parth I (God) will tell you about the Yogis who after death do not come back in this world and also about those who come back again after death."

The Lord is explaining to Arjun about life and death. Those who get Mokshya and those who come back again in the world.

अग्निर्ज्योतिरह: शुक्ल: षण्मासा उत्तरायणम् ।
तत्र प्रयाता गच्छन्ति ब्रह्म ब्रह्मविदो जना: ॥ (VIII-24) ॥

धूमो रात्रिस्तथा कृष्णः षण्मासा दक्षिणायनम् ।
तत्र चान्द्रमसं ज्योतिर्योगी प्राप्य निवर्तते ॥ (VIII-25) ॥

"O Arjun a devotee dying during light and during Uttarayana *i.e.*, when the Sun traverses the northern hemisphere goes to heaven and gets Moksha, he will not come back and goes for ever to God. The devotee who leaves this world in dark and dakshinayana *i.e.*, when the Sun traverses the southern hemisphere takes the path of moon light and goes to heaven. But after sometime has to take birth again and comes back in this world."

A pure saint has full control on his breaths and can leave his body at will. The typical example is of Bhishma. He was critically injured during the battle but did not die for so many days. He left his body only when he wanted to leave the same.

शुक्लकृष्णे गती होते जगतः शाश्वते मते ।
एकया यात्यनावृात्ति मन्यया वर्तते पुनः ॥ (VIII-26) ॥

"O Arjun these two paths of light (Shukla) and darkness (Krishna) coexist side by side from the time immemorial. Those who leave the universe in the light period attain Mokshya and go to the heaven permanently and others who leave during the dark period though go to heaven but come back in this world."

नैते सृती पार्थ जानन्योगी मुह्याति कश्चन ।
तस्मात्सर्वेषु कालेषु योगयुक्तो भवार्जुन ॥ (VIII-27) ॥

Krishna says "O Parth (Arjun) no Yogi who has understood regarding these two paths will ever deviate from the spiritual path. You are also a Yogi as such you will also take the right path to achieve salvation."

वेदेषु यज्ञेषु तपः सु चैव, दानेषु यत्पुण्यफलं प्रदिष्टम् ।
अत्येति तत्सर्वमिद विदित्वा, योगी परंस्थानमुपैति चाद्यम् ॥ (VIII-28) ॥

"O Arjun the Yogi who has clearly understood this secret about these two paths is even above those who are doing Yajnas penances and the study of Vedas, because he has understood the secret of life and death, and attains Moksha."

CHAPTER IX

Krishna is Explaining to Arjun about the Spiritual Knowledge and the Almighty (God)

इदं तु ते गुह्यतम प्रवक्ष्याम्यनसूयवे ।

ज्ञानं विज्ञानसहितं यज्ज्ञात्वा मोक्षसेऽशुभात् ॥ (IX-1) ॥

Lord Krishna says "O Arjun you are my best disciple and have come to me without any expectations. Therefore I will reveal to you the secrets of the knowledge, after understanding this you will not need any other knowledge, because this is the supreme and there is nothing beyond this."

Krishna still feels that Arjun is hiding some suspicions or confusion in his mind, therefore he wants to remove those conflicting thoughts from his mind.

राजविद्या राजगुह्यं पवित्रमिदमुत्तमम ।

प्रत्यक्षावगमं धर्म्यं सुसुखं कर्तुमव्ययम् ॥ (IX-2) ॥

अश्रद्धधाना: पुरूषा धर्मस्यास्य परतंप ।

अप्राप्य मां निर्वतन्ते मृत्युसंसारवर्त्मनि ॥ (IX-3) ॥

"O Arjun this spiritual knowledge is very sublime and sacred. I am giving you the same because there is an urge in you to gain it. Only who has faith and trust in God he can get this knowledge. Those who do not have faith, they are unable to attain it, and they keep on coming and going on this earth."

Krishna is explaining to Arjun that a devotee must have confidence and faith in the power supreme (God) to attain the spiritual knowledge which takes him out of the cycle of births and deaths. There should be an urge in the devotee for the same.

मया ततमिंद सर्वं जगदव्यक्त मूर्तिना ।

मत्स्थानि सर्व भूतानि न चाहं तेष्ववस्थित: ॥ (IX-4) ॥

न च मत्स्थानि भूतानि यश्च मे योगमैश्वरम् ।

भूतभृन्न च भूतस्थो ममात्मा भूतभावनः ॥ (IX-5) ॥

"The whole universe is in God as water is present in snow. All the mankind is in my body or within me but I (God) am not in all of them. I am (God) the creator as well as the destroyer of this universe."

The Lord says that though He (God) creates everything in this universe but it is not necessary that He may reside in each and every body. As the Sun, it has so many rays but it is not present in the rays itself. God only resides in pious and saintly persons.

यथाकाशस्थितो नित्यं वायुः सर्वत्रगो महान् ।

तथा सर्वाणि भूतानि मत्स्थानीत्युपधारय ॥ (IX-6) ॥

सर्वभूतानि कौन्तेय प्रकृतिं यान्ति मामिकाम् ।

कल्पक्षये पुनस्तानि कल्पादौ विसृजाम्यहम् ॥ (IX-7) ॥

Krishna says "O Kaunteya (Arjun) as the air in the atmosphere remains there throughout, in the same way all the people produced by nature (God) remain near the Almighty all the time. And when the end comes they go to the abode of God."

प्रकृतिं स्वामवष्टभ्य विसृजामि पुनः पुनः ।

भूतग्राममिमं कृत्स्नमवंश प्रकृतेर्वशात् ॥ (IX-8) ॥

न च मां तानि कर्माणि निबध्नन्ति धनंजय ।

उदासीनवदा सीन मसक्तं तेषु कर्मसु ॥ (IX-9) ॥

"O Dhananjaya (Arjun) and they are reborn according to their Karmas (deeds). I (God) am not attached to anybody but all the creatures come to Me (God) finally and are reborn according to the good or bad they have done in the provious birth.

मयाध्यक्षेण प्रकृतिः सूयते सचराचरम् ।

हेतुनानेन कौन्तेय जगद्विपरिवर्तते ॥ (IX-10) ॥

"O son of Kunti (Arjun) this universe is created by Me (God) with My Maya (creations) and also destroyed by Me from time to time. This cycle is going on regularly. This has been happening for the last so many yugas and will keep on happening in the future as well."

अवजानन्ति मां मूढा मानुषीं तनुमाश्रितम ।

परं भावमजान्नतो मम भूतमहेश्वरम् ।। (IX-11) ।।

मोघाशा मोघकर्माणो मोघज्ञानां विचेतसः ।

राक्षसीमासुरीं चैव प्रकृतिमोहिनीं श्रिताः ।। (IX-12) ।।

"But the people with negative attitude and lecherous tendencies cannot understand Me (God). I come in the form of human being with my Maya (divine power) to help pure from time to time, only saintly people can recognise Me, but those people who are bound by negative tendencies Tamsik Karma, anger, greed, attachments, ego, hatred, jealousy, cannot recognize Me. They are always surrounded by evil forces which bar them."

The Lord is explaining to Arjun that God does come on this earth in the shape of a human being to help the pious persons and the people with negative attitude in life cannot feel Gods presence amongst them.

महात्मानस्तु मां पार्थ दैवीं प्रकृतिमाश्रिताः ।

भजन्त्यनन्यमनसो ज्ञात्वा भूतादिमव्ययम् ।। (IX-13) ।।

सतंत कीर्तयन्तो मां यतन्तश्च दृढव्रताः ।

नमस्यन्तश्च मां भक्त्या नित्युक्ता उपासते ।। (IX-14) ।।

"O Arjun the saintly people always keep Me (God) in their thoughts. They perform noble actions in this world, Naturally these type of people are always close to Me. I give them my love. They worship Me and spread the spiritual knowledge to the rest."

ज्ञानयज्ञेन चाप्यन्ये यजन्तो मामुपासते ।

एकत्वेन पृथकत्वेन बहुधा विश्वतोमुखम् ।। (IX-15) ।।

"Some people worship Me by spreading my knowledge to the mankind. Some worship Me without any image. All the noble people are busy worshipping Me through different ways. They are always near to my heart and I show them the right path. They are doing good for themselves as well as for others and busy in the spiritual work. They not only live noble lives but also show the way to the rest of mankind to do the same."

अहं क्रतुरहं यज्ञः स्वधाहमहमौषधम् ।

मन्त्रोऽहमहमेवाज्यमहमग्निरहं हुतम् ॥ (IX-16) ॥

पिताहमस्य जगतो माता धाता पितामहः ।

वेद्यं पवित्रमोंकार ऋक्साम यजुरेव च ॥ (IX-17) ॥

"O Arjun I am present in all the creations, in this universe. I reside in all the human beings and the noble work done by them, the Yajnas done by them, the food given by them to their ancestors, the mantras recited during Yajnas, I reside in the Vedas. I am the mother, father and grand father of the whole mankind. I reside in the fire, oil and wooden pieces used in Havans performed by my devotees."

गतिर्भर्ता प्रभुः साक्षी निवासः शरणं सुहृत् ।

प्रभवः प्रलयः स्थानं निधानं बीजमव्ययम् ॥ (IX-18) ॥

तपाम्यहमंह वर्षं निगृह्णाम्युत्सृजामि च ।

अमृतं चैव मृत्युश्च सदसच्चाह मर्जुन ॥ (IX-19) ॥

"O Arjun I am the driving force in all the living and non-living creations. The whole universe is moving because of Me. I am in the Sun, in rainwater and in the moon. I am the sacred fire in Yajnas. All the births and deaths are as per my orders. I am immortal and look after all the mankind."

In short, Krishna is explaining to Arjun that God is omni-present, omniscient and omnipotent.

त्रिविद्या मां सोमपाः पूतपापा यज्ञैरिष्ट्वा सर्वगतिं प्रार्थयन्ते ।
ते पुण्यमासाद्य सुरेन्द्रलोग मश्नन्ति दिव्यान्दिवि देवभोगान् ॥ (IX-20) ॥

"O Arjun who believe in the Vedas and perform the deeds according to them are noble persons. They lead themselves towards heaven by their pious deeds."

ते तं भुक्त्वा स्वर्गलोकं विशालं क्षीणे पुण्ये मर्त्यलोकं विशन्ति ।
एवं त्रयोधर्ममनुप्रपन्ना गतागंत कामकामा लभन्ते ॥ (IX-21) ॥

"After their sojourn in the heaven, they come to the earth again and spend the rest of their lives in happiness and contentment. But those who do not believe in the Vedas live the lives in sorrow and difficulties, and they are restless and remain in tension throughout the existence."

Krishna is making clear to Arjun that those people who remain in touch with God have not to suffer anymore. They are happy here as well as in the heaven and ultimately blessed with salvation or Mokshya *i.e.*, total freedom.

अनन्याश्चिन्तयन्तो मां ये जनाः पर्युपासते ।
तेषां नित्याभियुक्तानां योगक्षेमं वहाम्यहम् ॥ (IX-22) ॥

Krishna says to Arjun "I take the responsibility of the devotee who comes to Me with faith, devotion and sincerity. I see that he does not fall, I become his protector against all the negatives in his life."

This is very significiant verse in Gita. The Lord gives assurance to his devotees that they should not worry once they have come to him. The God will protect them from all the difficulties. This is really a great promise. The devotee is rest assured that the Lord is by his side. Therefore he gets confidence and faces the life's challenges with courage and positive attitude.

येऽप्यन्यदेवता भक्ता यजन्ते श्रद्धयान्विताः ।
तेऽपि मामेव कौन्तेय यजन्त्यविधिपूर्वकम् ॥ (IX-23) ॥

Krishna says "O son of Kunti those who worship other Gods they are also worshipping me indirectly. They also in the final come to me for salvation or Mokshya."

As we know that God is one. So whatever path one chooses the final destination or the goal is the same for all.

अहं हि सर्वयज्ञानां भोक्ता च प्रभुरेव च ।
न तु मामभिजानन्ति तत्त्वेनातश्च्यवन्ति ते ।। 24 ।।

"The offerings and the Yajnas performed by the devotees come to Me. In return I (God) bless them with happiness and defend them from all the evil forces. I love my devotees and look after them. But those people who do not understand me, they are condemned and find themselves entrapped in the cycle of births and deaths and do not get salvation or Mokshya."

यान्ति देवव्रता देवान्पितॄन्यान्ति पितृव्रताः ।
भूतानि यान्ति भूतेज्या यान्ति मद्याजिनोऽपिमाम् ।। (IX-25) ।।

Krishna says "O Arjun those who worship lesser Gods they go to them, those who worship ancestors go to them, those who worship ghosts become ghosts but O Arjun those who worship Me they come to Me and I give them complete happiness and salvation. They come out the cycle of births and deaths and go to the abode of God *i.e.*, heaven."

पत्र पुष्पं फलं तोयं यो मे भक्त्याप्रयच्छति ।
तदहं भक्त्युपहृतमश्नामि प्रयतात्मनः।। (IX-26) ।।

Lord Krishna says "O Arjun my worship is very simple I do not demand anything from my devotee whatsoever is offered *i.e.*, leaves, flowers, fruits or water I accept the same with open arms. In return I give blessings, happiness and salvation to my devotee and a sense of fulfillment. The devotee who comes to me with faith and trust I take him under my protection."

यत्करोषि यदश्नासि यज्जुहोषि ददासि यत् ।
यत्तपस्यसि कौन्तेय तत्कुरूष्य मर्दपणम् ।। (IX-27) ।।

"Therefore O Arjun whatever you offer to God it comes to Me. Whatever, any Karma is done by you, any offering made, any Yajna is performed offer all to Me. This will give you a sense of satisfaction."

शुभाशुभ फलैरेवं मोक्ष्यसे कर्मबन्धनै ।
संन्यासयोगयुक्तात्मा विमुक्तों मामुपैष्यसि ॥ (IX-28) ॥

"O Arjun by surrendering all your Karmas to Me (God) you will become a saint or Yogi. You will be above all the bondages of this life, free yourself from the negative tendencies and this will pave the way for your salvation or Mukti."

समोऽहं सर्वभूतेषु न मे द्वेष्योऽस्ति न प्रियः ।
ये भजन्ति तु मां भक्त्या मयि ते तेषु चाप्यहम् ॥ (IX-29) ॥

"I am not friend of anyone nor I am the enemy. All the creations good or bad are immaterial to Me. But the devotee who worship Me without any rewards or expectations, my presence will always be in him."

अपि चेत्सुदुराचारो भजते मामनन्य भाक् ।
साधुरेव स मन्तव्यः सम्यग्व्य वसितो हि सः ॥ (IX-30) ॥

"O Arjun listen, even if a bad person starts worshipping me, I forgive him of his sins and accept him in my fold."

The Lord tells Arjun that even an evil person can become good and saintly, he can reform himself and become a noble person. We have seen many such examples where even criminals have become noble and pious persons.

क्षिप्रं भवति धर्मात्मा शश्वच्छान्तिं निगच्छति ।
कौन्तेय प्रति जानीहि न मे भक्तः प्रणश्यति ॥ (IX-31) ॥

"O son of Kunti, even the evil person who leaves sins and wants to become truthful I grant blessings to him. He can also become noble provided he has the will and determination to reform himself. If he shuns evil and takes the noble path."

The Lord explains to Arjun that not only the noble but even the evil person can get salvation as well if he leaves the negative tendencies in him.

मां हि पार्थ व्ययाश्रित्य येऽपि स्युः पापयोनयः ।
स्त्रियो वैश्यास्तथा शुद्रास्तेऽपि यान्ति परां गतिम् ॥ (IX-32) ॥

किं पुनर्ब्राह्मणाः पुण्या भक्ता राजर्षस्तथा ।
अनित्यमसुखं लोकमिमं प्राप्य भजस्व माम् ॥ (IX-33) ॥

"There is no discrimination in the abode of God, whether man, woman, Brahmin, Vaisha or Shudra all are equal and get salvation or Mokshya. He who worships Him with trust and faith God accepts him. Even the criminals can also reach him after shunning crime and going at the alter of God with clear, pious and truthful thoughts to escape from the cycle of births and deaths and attain Mokshya."

The doors of God are open to each and every person provided he has the desire and faith to reach Him.

मन्मना भव मद्भक्तो मद्याजी मां नमस्कुरू ।

मामेवैष्यसि युक्त्वैवमात्मानं मत्परायणः ॥ (IX-34) ॥

"The person who comes to me for salvation or Mokshya I do not disappoint him at all. He can live the life happily and leaves this earth for heaven, as such his both wrolds *i.e.*, on earth and in heaven are spent happily and attains Mokshya. So Arjun my advice to you is to go under the protection of the Almighty, who will remove all your difficulties and worries."

Lord Krishna is advising Arjun to have faith and confidence in God and leave all worries to Him. The God will definitely respond to your worship and remove your difficulties and obstacles.

CHAPTER X

In this Chapter Krishna is Explaining about the Power Supreme (God) and His Powers

भूय एव महाबाहो श्रृणु मे परमं वचः ।
यत्तेऽहं प्रोयमाणाय वक्ष्यामि हितकाम्यया ।। (X-1) ।।

"O Arjun I will now tell you in detail about the powers of God, listen to me carefully, as you are dear to me I am informing you the same. I will give the full picture, after this, all the confusions and negative tendencies will vanish from your mind."

न मे विदुः सुरगणाः प्रभवं न महर्षयः ।
अहमादिर्हि देवानां महर्षीणां च सर्वशः ।। (X-2) ।।

"No body knows about my origin, not even the minor gods and sages. All the mankind, living or non-living are in this universe because of Me. I have produced all of them, therefore they do not have any knowledge regarding My origin."

यो मामजमनादिं च वेत्ति लोक महेश्वरम् ।
असंमूढः स मर्त्येषु सर्वपापैः प्रमुच्यते ।। (X-3) ।।

"Those people who understand me, they know that I am eternal without any start or end. They become pious and full of positive attitude. They free themselves from the cycle of births and deaths. I am present throughout the universe and undistructiable." (I denotes God).

बुद्धिर्ज्ञानमस्मोहः क्षमां सत्यं दमः शमः ।
सुखं दुःखं भवोऽभावो भयं चाभयमेव च ।। (X-4) ।।
अहिंसा समता तुष्टिस्तपो दानं यशोऽयशः ।
भवन्ति भावा भूतानां मत्त एव पृथग्विधाः ।। (X-5) ।।

"All the traits of wisdom, knowledge, forgiveness, truth, happiness, unhappiness, fear, joy or sorrow, courage, charity, glory etc. are given by God to an individual."

In short all the traits in human beings are the gift of God

to them. A person exploits them as per his judgement and the degree of its acceptance or rejection.

महर्षयः सप्त पूर्वे चत्वारो मनवस्तथा ।
मद्भावा मानसा जाता येषां लोक इमाः प्रजाः ।। (X-6) ।।

"The whole mankind is the descendent of seven sages or rishis who in turn were created by God."

In other words, God is the creator of this universe including this earth. All those born on this, human beings or animals or plants are all the creations of God. In a nutshell, the Lord wants to empress upon Arjun that God is the creator as well as the destroyer of this world.

एतां विभूतिं योगं च मम यो वेत्ति तत्त्वतः ।
सोऽविकम्पेन योगेन युज्यते नात्र संशयः ।। (X-10) ।।

"O Arjun, a devotee who understands this *i.e.*, My Yogmaya, attains salvation or Mokshya and complete peace of mind. Thus he is able to come to My abode with his faith and trust in Me."

अहं सर्वस्य प्रभवो मत्तः सर्वं प्रवर्तते ।
इति मत्वा भजन्ते मां बुधा भावसमन्विताः ।। (X-8) ।।
मच्चित्ता मद्गतप्राणा बोधयन्तः परस्परम् ।
कथयन्तश्च मां नित्यं तुष्यन्ति च रमन्ति च ।। (X-9) ।।
तेषां सततयुक्तानां भजतां प्रीतिपूर्वकम् ।
ददामि बुद्धियोगं तं येन मामुपयान्ति ते ।। (X-10) ।।

"The devotees who know that I (God) am the maker of this universe, they do not have any doubt in Me and My creations. They put their faith in Me and I do not fail them and bless them with the gift of Contentment and peace of mind. They feel themselves in complete peace of mind and always find themselves under My protection."

Here I and Me, My etc. denote God.

तेषामेवानुकम्पार्थमहमज्ञानन्जं तमः ।
नाशयाम्यात्मभावस्थो ज्ञानदीपेन भास्वता ।। (X-11) ।।

"The persons who come to Me. I destroy their fears in their lives and take them towards light and happiness. There should be no doubt regarding the same in My devotees."

After listening to Krishna, Arjun says "O Lord" :

परं ब्रह्म परं धाम पवित्रं परमं भवान् ।
पुरूष शाश्वंत दिव्यमादिदेवमजं विभुम् ॥ (X-12) ॥

"O Krishna you are supreme, most powerful and sacred. You are higher of the highest and purer of the purest. I bow with respect to you."

आहुस्त्वामृषयः सर्वे देवर्षिर्नारदस्तथा ।
असितो देवलो व्यासः स्वयं चैव ब्रवीषि मे ॥ (X-13) ॥
सर्वमेतदृतं मन्ये यन्मां वदसि केशव ।
न हिते भगवन्वयक्ति विदुर्देवा न दानवाः ॥ (X-14) ॥
स्वयमेवात्मनात्मानं वेत्थ त्वं पुरूषोत्तम ।
भूतभावन भूतेश देवदेव जगत्पते ॥ (X-15) ॥

"O Krishna, sages like Narada, Asita, Devala and above all even sage Vedvyasa have said the same thing about you and your supernatural powers. O Krishna no one *i.e.*, human beings and demons have seen your multidimensional form, so far also believe that the same is true. You are supreme and the creator of this universe."

So we see here that now Arjun is convinced that the Lord (Krishna) is supreme and whatever God has said to him is correct. When one becomes clear in his mind the doubts and confusions fade way.

वक्तु मर्हस्य शेषेण दिव्या ह्यात्मविभूतयः ।
याभिर्विभूतिभिर्लो कानिमांस्त्वं व्याप्य तिष्ठसि ॥ (X-16) ॥
कथं विद्यामहं योगिस्त्विां सदा परिचिन्तयन् ।
केषु केषु च भावेषु चिन्तयोऽसि भगवन्मया ॥ (X-17) ॥
विस्तरेणात्मनो योगं विभूतिं च जर्नादन ।
भूयः कथय तृप्तिर्हि श्रृण्वतो नास्ति मेऽमृत्म् ॥ (X-18) ॥

O Krishna you are present everywhere in this universe and the creator of everything on this earth. Please let me know about the yogic powers you talked about. I want to get knowledge about this Yogmaya with which you have created this universe. O Lord you are omnipresent, omniscient and omnipotent and have created this universe. Please let me know in detail as to how you have created this world with your cosmic strength or Yogmaya. I am not clear in my mind regarding all this, therefore I request you to put some light on it."

हन्त ते कथयिष्यामि दिव्या ह्यात्मविभूतयः ।
प्राधान्यतः कुरूश्रेष्ठ नास्त्यन्तो विस्तरस्य मे ।। (X-19) ।।
अहमात्मा गुडाकेश सर्वभूताशयस्थितः ।
अहमादिश्च मध्यं च भूतानामन्त एव च ।। (X-20) ।।

O Arjun since you want to know more about my divine powers or dimensions I will let you know all about the same Soul is the main centre in the human body. I (God) am the beginning, the middle and the end in nature. I am present everywhere throughout the universe.

आदित्यानामहं विष्णुर्ज्योतिषां रविंरशुमान् ।
मरीचिर्मरूतामस्मि नक्षत्राणामहं शशी ।। (X-21) ।।

I am Vishnu amongst Gods, amongst the heavenly bodies I am the Sun, in the wind Gods I am Mareechi, amongst the Stars I am the moon. I am present everywhere.

वेदानां सामवेदोऽस्मि देवानामस्मि वासवः ।
इन्द्रियाणां मनश्चास्मि भूवानामस्मि चेतना ।। (X-22) ।।
रूद्राणां शंकरश्चास्मि वित्तेशो यक्षरक्षसाम् ।
वसूनां पावकश्चास्मि मेरूः शिखरिणामहम् ।। (X-23) ।।

I am Samveda among the Vedas. Amongst the Gods I am Indra. In the whole body I am the heart and in the conscience I am the intelligence. Amongst the Rudras I am Shiva, among rasas I am fire and amongst the peaks I am Sumeru peak.

पुरोधसां च मुख्यं मां विद्धि पार्थ बृहस्पतिम् ।
सेनानीनांमहं स्कन्दः सरसामस्मि सागरः ।। (X-24) ।।
महर्षीणां भृगुरंह गिरामस्म्येकमक्षरम् ।
यज्ञानां जपयज्ञोऽस्मि स्थावराणां हिमालयः ।। (X-25) ।।

O Parth says Krishna amongst priests I am Brihaspati, in the commanders I am Skanda, in water bodies I am the Sea. Amongst sages I am Bhrigu, amongst the words I am 'OM', amongst the Yajnas I am Japa Yajna and amongst mountains I am Himalaya the tallest.

अश्वत्थः सर्ववृक्षाणां देवर्षीणां च नारदः ।
गन्धर्वाणां चित्ररथः सिद्धानां कपिलो मुनिः ॥ (X-26) ॥
उच्चैः श्रवसमश्वानां विद्धि माममृतोभ्दवम् ।
ऐरावतं गजेन्द्राणां नराणां च नराधिपम् ॥ (X-27) ॥
आयुधानामहं वज्रं धेनूनामस्मि कामधुक् ।
प्रजनश्चास्मि कन्दर्पः सर्पाणामस्मि वासुकिः ॥ (X-28) ॥

Among the trees I am the peepal tree, among the devrishes I am Narada Muni, among the learned people I am Kapila Muni, among the horses I am the sacred Uchcheshrava horse. I am the king among the people. I am Kama from all the desires. Among the weapons of destruction I am Vajra, among the cows I am Kamdhenu, the most sacred cow and among the snakes I am the Vasuki snake.

अनन्तश्चास्मि नागानां वरूणो यादसामहम् ।
पितृणामर्यमा चास्मि यमः संयमतामहम् ॥ (X-29) ॥
प्रह्लादश्चास्मि दैत्यानां कालः कलयतामहम् ।
मृगाणां च मृगेन्द्रोऽहं वैनतेयश्च पक्षिणाम् ॥ (X-30) ॥
पवनः पवतामस्मि रामः शस्त्रभृतामहम ।
झषाणां मकरश्चास्मि स्त्रोतसामस्मि जाह्नवो ॥ (X-31) ॥
सर्गाणामदिरन्तश्च मध्यं चैवाहमर्जुन ।
अध्यात्मविद्या विद्यानां वादः प्रवदतामहम् ॥ (X-32) ॥

Among the cobras (deadly snakes) I am the Shesh Nag. Among the water creatures I am Varna. Among the ancestors I am Ayarma, among the rulers I am Yama, among the demons I am Prahalada Bhagat.

Among the measures I am Time, among the birds I am Garuda, among the purifiers I am wind, among the warriors I am Rama among the fish I am Crocodile. Among the rivers I am the most sacred Ganga.

Among the knowledge I am the spiritual science and among the speakers I am the winner. O Arjun I (God) am present everywhere in this universe. I am (God) is the greater of the greatest.

अक्षराणामकारोऽस्मि द्वन्द्वः सामासिकस्च च ।

अहमेवाक्षःय कालो धाताहं विश्वतोमुखः ।। (X-33) ।।

मृत्युः सर्वहरश्चाहमुद्भवश्च भविष्यताम् ।

कीर्तिः श्रीर्वाक्च नारीणां स्मृतिमेर्धा धृतिः क्षमा ।। (X-34) ।।

You will find me in all the knowledge books I am timeless with no beginning or end. I am looking after everyone on this earth. I am the Lord of death and takes the person away from the earth when the time of death comes. I am the provider of Fame, Memory, intelligence, prosperity, courage, pardon, etc. I am the beauty and glory in mankind.

बृहत्साम तथा साम्नां गायत्री छन्दसामहम ।

मासानां मार्गशीर्षोऽहमृतूनां कुसुमाकरः ।। (X-35) ।।

द्यूतं छलयतामस्मि तेजस्तेजस्विनामहम् ।

जयोऽस्मि व्यवसायोऽस्मि सत्वं सत्त्ववतामहम् ।। (X-36) ।।

वृष्णीनां वासुदेवोऽस्मि, पाण्डवानां धनंजयः ।

मुनीनामप्यहं व्यासः कवीनामुशना कविः ।। (X-37) ।।

In the hymns I am Brihatsam. In couplets I am Gayatri Mantra, the most sacred of all the couplets, in the month I am Margshirsha and in the seasons I am the most beautiful of all *i.e.*, spring. In deception I am gamble. I am winner in victory, the verdict of the judges and nobility of the noble. In gods I am Vasudev and Arjun (Dhananjay) in Pandavas, in the learned people I am Vedvyasa and in poets I am Shukracharya.

दण्डो दमयतामस्मि नीतिरस्मि जिगीषताम् ।
मौनं चैवास्मि गुह्यानां ज्ञानं ज्ञानवतामहम् ।। (X-38) ।।
यच्चापि सर्वभूतानां बीजं तदहमर्जुन ।
न तदस्ति विना यत्स्यान्मया भूतं चराचरम् ।। (X-39) ।।

O Arjun I am the arrogance of the oppnessors, planning of the Victors, silence of the those who keep secrets, knowledge of the learned people, I am the one who gives birth to the living beings. The past was due to me, the present is due to me and the future will also be due to me. In short, I am the prime mover of this universe.

(I or me stands for God the Almighty)

नान्तोऽस्ति मम दिव्यानां विभूतीनां परंतप ।
एष तूद्देशत: प्रोक्तो विभूतेर्विस्तरो मया ।। (X-40) ।।

O Arjun my powers are limitless, but in brief I have told you about the same. I am without any limits and present in all the living and non-living and guide them in all their deeds through brain given to the living by Me.

यद्यद्विभूतिमत्सत्त्वं श्रीमदूर्जितमेव वा ।
तत्तदेवावगच्छत्वं मम तेजोंऽशसम्भवम् ।। (X-41) ।।
अथवा बहुनैतेन किं ज्ञातेन तवार्जुन ।
विष्टभ्याहमिदं कृत्स्नमेकांशेन स्थितो जगत् ।। (X-42) ।।

O Arjun all the things which are shinning or glowing, pleasing they all have a part of mine in them. I give them all the energy to survive in the universe.

O Arjun why you want to know more about this phenomenon? All the universe has been made by Me with my Yogmaya I am the Creator of this universe with my powers. This will go on for ever and there is no limit to that.

The Lord (Krishna) is explaining to Arjun that God is the maker and destroyer of this universe. People will keep on coming and going from here from time to time. This has been happening from the time immemorial and will keep on happening in the future as well. In short, God is omnipresent, omniscient and omnipotent. Without His will nothing can happen in this universe.

CHAPTER XI

Krishna is Explaining to Arjun Regarding the Powers of Almighty (God). He Shows his Divine Form to Arjun in this Chapter

मदनुग्राहाय परमं गुह्यमंध्यात्म संज्ञितम् ।
यत्त्वयोक्तं वचस्तेन मोहोऽयं विगतो मम ।। (XI-1) ।।

Arjun says to Lord Krishna, O Lord with your explanation my doubts have been cleared and now I can understand what you wanted to explain to me. My doubts are no more and I can see and think clearly and with positive attitude what you desired.

Arjun is no more dejected and now he could speak with confidence. The Lord had shown him the way with details. Arjun is happy now and thankful to Krishna.

भवाप्ययौ हि भूतानां श्रुतौ विस्तरशो मया ।
त्वत्तः कमलपत्राक्ष माहात्म्यमपि चाव्ययम् ।। (XI-2) ।।

O Lord what you explained about the life and death has been understood by me. I know that you are the creator and destroyer of this universe.

Arjun has now clearly understood that only God is the power supreme behind all this universe and whatever is happening in this world is by the grace of God. Nothing can happen without his knowledge and the Almighty is present everywhere. All are his creations.

एवमेतद्यथात्थ त्वमात्मांन परमेश्वर ।
द्रष्टुमिच्छामि ते रूपपैश्वरं पुरूषोत्तम ।। (XI-3) ।।
मन्यसे यदि तच्छंक्यं मया द्रष्टुमिति प्रभो ।
योगेश्वर ततो मे त्वं दर्शयात्मानमव्ययम् ।। (XI-4) ।।

O Krishna what you have said is right. You have the divine powers. I am eager to see your divine form. If you feel that I deserve to see your original and divine form then I request you to let me see your pious original and divine form.

Arjun is convinced here that the God has come on the

earth in the form of a human being *i.e.*, Krishna. Therefore, he is curious to see that form of the power supreme, which he is unable to see so far. That is why he requests Lord Krishna to reveal him the real face or the true form of the Almighty.

पश्य मे पार्थ रूपाणि शतशोऽथ सहस्त्रश: ।
नानाविद्यानि दिव्यानि नानावर्णाकृतीनि च ।। (XI-5) ।।

O Parth (Arjun) as desired by you I will show you my divine form, get ready to see which consists of thousands of heads, arms and an enormous body, who is the creator of this universe and the destroyer as well.

Krishna had already shown his divine power earlier as well (*a*) to his friends Akroora in the river Yamuna by mounting on the Nagraj (Snake) and taming the same. (*b*) to his mother Yashoda when he was a child. She scolded him and asked him to open the mouth to check if Krishna had eaten the mud or not. To her utter surprise she found the entire universe in his mouth revolving like a little ball. (*c*) in the court of Kaurvas when he came to the rescue of Draupadi and saved her from dishonour.

पश्यादित्यान्वसून्रूद्रानश्विनौ मरूतस्तथा ।
बहून्यदृष्टपूर्वाणि पश्याश्र्याणि भारत ।। (XI-6) ।।

O Bharat (Arjun) you will see in my this divine form twelve sons of Aditi, eight Vasus, fortynine gods of wind, eleven rudras and so many other stange and wonderful sights you have not witnessed ever before.

इहैकस्थं जगत्कृत्स्नं पश्याद्य सचराचरम् ।
मम देहे गडाकेश यच्चान्यद् द्रष्टुमिच्छसि ।। (XI-7) ।।

O Gudakesh (Arjun-Conqueror of sleep) you will see my divine form hitherto not imagined by anyone. You can see the entire cosmos or universe in my this massive body.

God does not have any particular shape or body, but the devotees can see him in what so ever form they want or wish to see.

न तु मां शक्यसे द्रष्टुमनेनैव स्वचक्षुषा ।
दिव्यं ददामि ते चक्षुः पश्य मे योगमैश्वरम् ॥ (XI-8) ॥

O Arjun you will not be able to witness this cosmic and divine vision with your ordinary eye sight. Therefore I bless and grant you divine sight so that you are in a position to see this cosmic vision of my divine form.

After this the Lord grants the devine vision to Arjun to see the divine form.

एवमुक्त्वा ततो राजन्महायोगेश्वरो हरिः ।
दर्शयामास पार्थाय परमं रूपमैश्वरम ॥ (XI-9) ॥

Sanjay is narrating the events taking place in the battle field of Kurukshetra to king Dhrithrastra. He says O King at this point Lord Krishna revealed his divine form to Arjun.

अनेकवक्त्रनयन मनेकाद्भुतदर्शनम् ।
अनेकदिव्याभरणं दिव्यानेकोद्यतायुधम् ॥ (XI-10) ॥
दिव्यमाल्याम्बरधरं दिव्यगन्धानुलेपनम् ।
सर्वाश्चर्यमयं देवमनन्तं विश्वतोमुखम् ॥ (XI-11) ॥

At this point Arjun sees a massive structure with thousands of heads, thousands of arms and eyes, holding many fire arms. The structure was so enormous and awesome that Arjun becomes very terrified and perplexed at this unnatural sight.

दिवि सूर्यसहस्त्रस्य भवेद्युगपदुत्थिता ।
यदि भाः सदृशी सा स्याभ्दासस्तस्य महात्मनः ॥ (XI-12) ॥

The light emitting from the divine form is so bright and glowing that even the light of thousand of Suns cannot match the same.

तत्रैकस्थं जगत्कृत्स्नं प्रविभक्तमनेकधा ।
अपश्यद्देवदेवस्य शरीरे पाण्डवस्तदा ॥ (XI-13) ॥

Arjun (Son of Pandu) is perplexed to watch this spectacle of the power supreme (God). He is extremely nervous to see the entire universe standing in front of him.

ततः स विस्मयाविष्टो हृष्टरोमा धनंजयः ।
प्रणम्य शिरसा देवं कृतांजलिरभाषत ।। (XI-14) ।।

Arjun is very frightened to see this enormous structure standing in front of him. He could not believe his sight. He is extremely excited, bends down and pay his respects.

पश्यामि देवांस्तव देव देहे सर्वांस्तथां भूतविशेष संघान् ।
ब्रह्माणमीश कमलासनस्थमृषींश्च सर्वानुरगांश्च दिव्यान् ।। (XI-15) ।।

O Krishna I can see Brahma sitting on a lotus surrounded by many saints and Rishis. Your thousands of heads, eyes and arms. Some of the hands holding weapons of mass destruction. The sight is very awesome and stunning. I have not seen such a spectacle in my life ever before.

अनेकबाहूदरवक्त्रनेत्रं पश्यामि त्वां सर्वतोऽनन्तरूपम् ।
नान्तं न मध्यं न पुनस्तवादिं पश्यामि विश्वेश्वर विश्वरूप ।। (XI-16) ।।

O Lord I can see many faces, heads, arms and eyes. There seems to be no beginning or end of the same. It is such a huge structure. It is amazing to witness this extremely strange, awesome and incredible sight.

किरीटिंन गदिन चक्रिण. च तेजोराशि सर्वतो दीप्तिमन्तम् ।
पश्चामि त्वां दुर्निरीक्ष्यं समन्ता द्दीप्तान लार्कद्युतिमप्रमेयम् ।। (XI-17) ।।

There are countless crowns on your heads. Many destructive weapons being held by your many arms. The huge body (structure) is blazing like many Suns, I feel very terrified.

त्वमक्षंर परमं वेदितव्यं त्वमस्य विश्वस्य परं निधानम्।
त्वमव्ययशाश्वत्धर्मगोप्ता सनातनस्त्वं पुरूषो मतो मे ।। (XI-18) ।।

O Krishna I am convinced that you are imperishable, present throughout the universe and eternal. You are supreme and shelter the whole world in your body, protector of Dharma (religion) and immortal.

By watching the huge structure standing in front of him, Arjun is terrified and surprised. There are thousands of heads emitting fire engulfing the living and non-living bodies. On seeing this cosmic spectacle he is completely lost.

अनादिमध्यान्तमनन्त वीर्यं अन्तबांहु शशिसूर्यनेत्रम्।
पश्यामि त्वां दीप्तहुताशवक्त्रं स्वतेजसा विश्वमिंद तपन्तम् ।। (XI-19) ।।

You have no beginning or end I can see thousands of arms, heads and eyes. The Sun and the Moon are your eyes. Your mouths are emitting fire and I see innumerable creatures being engulfed by the fire coming out from your mouths. It is very horrifying scene to witness.

द्यावापृथिव्योरिदमन्तरं हि व्याप्तं त्वयैकेत दिशश्व सर्वाः।
दृष्टाद्भूतं रूपमुग्रं तवेदं लोकत्रंय प्रव्यथिंतं महात्मन् ।। (XI-20) ।।

O Lord your huge body is occupying the whole sky, right from heaven to earth. This scene I have never encountered throughout my life. It appears that you have occupied the entire space which is very threatening, horrible and unnatural.

अमी हि त्वां सुरसघां विशन्ति केचिद्भीताः प्रांजलयो गृणन्ति ।
स्वस्तीत्युकत्वा महर्षिसिद्धसंघाः स्तुवन्ति त्वां स्तुतिभिः पुष्कलाभिः ।। (XI-21) ।।

Scores of creatures both human and animals are being engulfed by your fire emitting ferocious mouths. Saints and sages are singing your prayers with folded hands. At this time the divine cosmic structure becomes dynamic *i.e.*, the moments start in the whole body and it start moving.

रूद्रादित्या वसवो ये च साध्या विश्वेऽश्विनौ मरूत श्चोष्मपाश्च ।
गन्धर्वयक्षासुरसिध्यसघां वीक्षन्ते त्वां विस्मिताश्चैव सर्वे ।। (XI-22) ।।

O Krishna I can also see so many others *i.e.*, the Rudras, Adityas, Vasus, Sadhyas, Viswedevas, Aswins, Maruts, the pitrus (ancestors), Gandharvas, Yakhas and Asuras, watching this cosmic and divine form with horror and astonishment.

रूपं महत्ते बहुवस्त्र नेत्रं महाबाहो बहुबाहूरूपादम् ।
बहूदरं बहुदंष्ट्राकरालं दृष्ट्वा लोकाः प्रव्यथितास्तथाहम् ।। (XI-23) ।।

It is awesome to see thousands of heads, arms, eyes, bellies of this divine structure. All the people who are watching are extremely terrified and full of horror. I am also very much disturbed and confused at this sight.

नभः स्पृशं दीप्तमनेकवर्णं व्यात्ताननं दोप्तविशालनेत्रम् ।
दृष्टवा हि त्वां प्रव्यथितान्तरात्मा धृतिं न विन्दामि शमं च विष्णो ॥ (XI-24) ॥

O Krishna your incredible, gigantic body, burning eyes, so many mouths make me afraid. I am very restless to witness this unnatural scene. I am very nervous at this sight.

दंष्ट्रा करालानि च ते मुखानि दृष्टैव कालानलसन्निभानि ।
दिशो न जाने न लभे च शर्म प्रसीद देवेश जगन्निवास ॥ (XI-25) ॥

O Lord I am very much afraid to see your big jaws emitting fire like some inferno. I cannot see this sight anymore. I am nervous and restless.

अमी च त्वां धृतराष्टस्य पुत्राः सर्वे सहैवावनिपालसंधैः ।
भीष्मो द्रोणसूत पुत्रस्तथासौ सहास्मदीयैरपि योधमुख्यैः ॥ (XI-26) ॥

I can see sons of Dhritrashtra and so many others kings including Bhishma Guru Dhrona, Karna and some others from our (family as well) entering your burning jaws. That is extremely horrible and frightening to watch.

वक्त्राणि ते त्वरमाणा विशन्ति दंष्ट्राकरालानि भयानकानि ।
केचिद्विलग्ना दशनान्तरेषु सन्दृश्यन्ते चूर्णितैरूत्त मांगैः ॥ (XI-27) ॥

I see many trapped between your fearsome jaws and many of them lying dead on the ground after escaping from them.

Here the Lord brings home to Arjun that those worriors on the Kaurvas side are going to perish. By depicting this scene God is ensuring Arjun that his (Pandavas) enemies are facing sure death, and there is no escape from this. Therefore Arjun should not worry as victory is sure and there should not be any doubt in the mind of Arjun. The proof of the same was in front of him.

यथा नदीनां बहवो ऽम्बु वेगाः समुद्रमेवाभिमुखा द्रवन्ति ।
तथा तवामी नरलोक वीरा विशन्ति वक्त्राण्यभिविज्वलन्ति ॥ (XI-28) ॥

As the rivers are fast running towards the sea to be absorbed by it, in the same way worriors of the Kaurvas army are also running towards your fire emitting jaws and getting destroyed.

यथा प्रदीप्तं ज्वलनं पतगां विशन्ति नाशाय समृद्धवेगा: ।
तथैव नाशाय विशन्ति लोका स्तवापि वक्त्राणि समृद्ध वेगा: ।। (XI-29) ।।

As the insects fly towards the flame to be destroyed ultimately, in the same way the worriors of the Kaurvas army are running into your burning jaws and getting destroyed.

लेलिह्यसे ग्रसमान: समन्ता ल्लोकान्समग्रान्वदनैर्ज्वलद्भि: ।
तेजोभिरापूर्य जगत्समग्रं भासस्त वोग्रा: प्रतपन्ति विष्णो ।। (XI-30) ।।

O Vishnu (Lord Krishna is also know as Vishnu).

You are chewing the soldiers of the Kaurvas army with your dreadful jaws and tongues. The brightness and the heat of your body is engulfing the whole universe.

Lord Krishna is supposed to be the incarnation of Lord Vishnu, that is why Arjun is addressing Krishna as Lord Vishnu in this verse.

आख्याहि मे को भवानुग्ररूपो: नमोऽस्तु ते देववर प्रसीद ।
विज्ञातुमिच्छामि भवन्त माद्यं न हि प्रजानामि तव प्रवृत्तिम् ।। (XI-31) ।।

O Krishna I do not understand as to why you are in this dreadful form? Please let me know as to why you have transformed yourself in this awesome form? I am not able to understand about your mission in this. Please explain to me.

कालोऽस्मि लोकक्षय कृत्प्रवृद्धो: लोकान्समाहर्तुमिह प्रवृत्त: ।
ऋतेऽपित्वां न भविष्यन्ति सर्वे येऽवस्थिता: प्रत्यनीकेषु योधा: ।। (XI-32) ।।

Krishna says, O Arjun I am the maker as well as the destroyer of this universe. I am the Mahakaal (destroyer) and destroy this world from time to time and again revive the same. The persons you are seeing in the Kaurvas camp, do you think they are going to survive? Even if you do not fight they are already on the death roll. They will definitely die even if you do not kill them. Because their end has come.

तस्मात्त्वमुत्तिष्ठ यशो लभस्व जित्वा शत्रून् भुंक्ष्व राज्यं समृद्धम् ।
मयैवैते निहता: पूर्वमेव निमित्तमात्रं भव सव्यसाचिन् ।। (XI-33) ।।

Therefore get up and kill all the opponents standing in front of you. You will get glory and reign the kingdom. Rest assure that all have already been killed by me (God) by my divine powers. They all are going to die even if you do not kill them.

द्रोणं च भीष्मं च जयद्रथं च कर्णं तथान्यानपि योधवीरान् ।
मया हतांस्त्वं जहि मा व्यथिष्ठाः युद्धस्व जेतासि रणे सपत्नान् ।। (XI-34) ।।

Therefore get up and kill them *i.e.*, Drona, Bhishma, Jayadrath, Karna and all the other worriors. They have already been killed by me by my divine powers. You have to do the formality of bringing them down victory will be yours.

Arjun had shown doubts in the beginning that what surety was there that they (Pandavas) would win or able to kill Kaurvas. The reverse could also happen. Here Lord Krishna gives surety and assurance to Arjun that victory would be their because he (Krishna) had already killed them with his divine powers.

एतच्छ्रुत्वा वचनं केशवस्य कृतांजलिर्वेपमानः किरीटी ।
नमस्कृत्वा भूय एवाह कृष्णं सगद्गदं भीतभीतः प्रणम्य ।। (XI-35) ।।

Sanjay is narrating the events taking place in the battle field of Kurukshetra to king Dhritrashtra. He says "O King on hearing the words of Krishna, Arjun becomes very nervous and terrified. He bends down with folded hands before Krishna and says as under."

स्थाने ऋषीकेश तव प्रकीर्त्या जगत्प्रहृष्यत्यनुरज्यते च ।
राक्षांसि भीतानि दिशो द्रवन्ति सर्वे नमस्यन्ति च सिद्धसंधाः ।। (XI-36) ।।

Arjun says to Lord Krishna "The whole mankind is paying respects to you. The enemy forces are running here and there for safety from your jaws. The pious and saintly people are singing your glory.

कस्माच्च ते न नमेरन्महात्मन् गरीयसे ब्रह्मणोऽप्यादिकर्त्रे ।
अनन्त देवेश जगन्निवास त्वमक्षरं सदसत्तत्परं यत् ।। (XI-37) ।।

O Lord you are the creator of this universe and even above Brahma, that is why all the gods also paying respects to you. You are the mightest and beyond the cycle of births and deaths you are the prime mover of this universe. You are imperishable and the Supreme God and prime force and authority.

त्वामाहिदेवः पुरूषः पुराणः स्त्वमस्य विश्वस्य परंनिधानम् ।
वेत्तासिवेद्यं च परं च धाम त्वया ततं विश्वमनन्तरूप ।। (XI-38) ।।

O Lord you have many forms and dimensions being the oldest in the whole of universe. You are the supreme refuge of the human beings and the others as well. You are present everywhere in the universe.

वायुर्यमोऽग्निर्वरूणशशांकः प्रजापतिस्त्वं प्रपिता महश्च ।
नमो नमस्तेऽस्तु सहस्त्र कृत्वः पुनश्च भूयोऽपि नमो नमस्ते ।। (XI-39) ।।

O Lord you are the god of wind, fire and death, the god of water and the moon god. I bow to you thousand times again and again because you are the creator as well as the destroyer of this world.

नमः पुरस्तादथ पृष्तस्ते नमोऽस्तु ते सर्वत एव सर्व ।
अन्नतवीर्यामित विक्रमस्त्वं सर्वं समाप्नोषि ततोऽसि सर्वः ।। (XI-40) ।।

I pay my respect to you. I salute you. You are all powerful on this earth.

सखेति मत्वा प्रसंभ यदुक्तं हे कृष्ण हे यादव हे सखेति ।
अजानता माहेमानं तवेदं मया प्रमादात्प्रणयेन वापि ।। (XI-41) ।।

O Krishna my friend, I might have spoken some words which you might not have liked. I ask for your pardon because it must have been my ignorance. I request for your forgiveness. I regret the same. Being my friend and well wisher I know you will definitely forgive me.

At this stage Arjun has realized that Krishna is not an ordinary person. He is an incarnation of God.

यच्चावहासार्थमस्त्कृतोऽसि विहारशय्यासनभोजनेषु ।
एकोऽथवाप्यच्युत तस्समक्षं तत्क्षमये त्वामहमप्रमेयम् ।। (XI-42) ।।

O Lord I might have hurt you with my thoughts and actions. I ask for your pardon because it might have happened due to an oversight and my ignorance. I regret the same very much. I hope to be forgiven by you as you love me and other worshippers too who have faith in you.

पितासि लोकस्य चराचरस्य त्वमस्य पूज्यश्च गुरूर्गरीयान् ।
न त्वत्समोऽस्त्यभ्यधिकः कुतोऽन्यो लोकत्रयेऽप्यप्रतिमप्रभाव ।। (XI-43) ।।

O Krishna you are just like father of this universe. No one can surpass your strength and divine powers. You are the master of the universe and omnipotent (all powerful).

तस्मात्प्रणम्य प्रणिधाय कायं प्रसादये त्वाम हमीशमीऽयम् ।
पितेव पुत्रस्य सखेव सख्युः प्रियः प्रियायार्हसि देव सोढुम् ।। (XI-44) ।।

O Lord like a father who pardons his sons for any wrong they have done. Similarly I am just like a son to you and you should forgive if I have done any disrespect to you. I love and have a great faith in you.

अद्रष्टपूर्व हृषितोऽस्मिदृष्ट्वा भयेन च प्रव्यथिंत मनो में ।
तदेव में दर्शय देवरूपं प्रसीद देवेश जगन्निवास ।। (XI-45) ।।

I have seen your divine form. I am really very much terrified and distressed to watch this awesome, incredible and gigantic form. I request you to come back into your original form smiling and having four arms (Vishnu). I will be pleased to see that form once again.

Lord Krishna is supposed to be the incarnation of Lord Vishnu. As Lord Vishnu is shown having four arms, therefore Arjun requested Lord Krishna to come back having four arms. The Lord had appeared having four arms earlier as well as depicted in the Bhagwat. That is why Arjun is requesting Krishna to come back in the form of Lord Vishnu.

किरीटिंन गदिंन चक्रहस्त मिच्छामि त्वां द्रष्टुमहं तथैव ।
तेनैव रूपेण चतुर्भुजेन सहस्त्रबाहो भव विश्वमूर्ते ।। (XI-46) ।।

O Lord I would like to see you in the original form once again holding mace and discuss in your arms. With crown on your head and with four arms. I request you to discard this awesome figure and show me your pleasant and sweet form once again.

It is said that Krishna appeared in four arms twice earlier as well. Once when he was born and again when he was teasing his wife Rukmani. She fell unconscious and to revive her he appeared in that form. Arjun must be knowing about this, as such he requested Krishna to appear with four arms.

मयाप्रसन्नेन तवार्जुनेदं रूपं परं दर्शितमात्मयोगात् ।
तेजोमयं विश्वमनन्तमाद्यं यन्मे त्वदन्येन न दृष्टपूर्वम् ॥ (XI-47) ॥

Krishna says "O Arjun I have shown you my this divine gigantic form because you are my disciple and close to me. I am pleased with your devotion. No one has seen this in the whole universe ever before.

न वेदयज्ञा ध्ययनैर्न दानैर्न च क्रियार्भिर्न तपोभिरूग्रैः ।
एवंरूपशक्य अहं नृलोके दृष्टुं त्वदन्येन कुरूप्रवीर ॥ (XI-48) ॥

O Arjun the divine spectacle you have just seen, no other could see the same inspite of the study of Vedas and worship. No one in this world has seen My this form ever before.

मा ते व्यथा मा च विमूढभावोः दृष्ट्वा रूपं घोरमोद्दडम मेदम् ।
व्यपेतंभीः प्रीतमना पुनस्त्वं तदेव मे रूपमिंद प्रपश्य ॥ (XI-49) ॥

You should not be afraid or terrified by witnessing my this unusual form. As requested by you I come back to my original form.

After this Krishna transformed himself in the original normal form once again.

इत्यर्जुनं वासुदेवस्तथोक्त्वा स्वकं रूपं दर्शयामास भूयः ।
आश्वासयामास च भीतमेनं भूत्वा पुनः सौम्यवपुर्महात्मा ॥ (XI-50) ॥

Sanjay is narrating the events taking place at the battle field of Kurukshetra to king Dhritrashtra. He says "O King after this Krishna transforms himself to his original natural form as before to console terror striken Arjun."

दृष्टेवदं मानुषं रूपं तव सौम्यं जनार्दन ।
इदानीमास्मि संवृत्तः सचेताः प्रकृतिं गतः ॥ (XI-51) ॥

Arjun says "O Krishna I am happy to see you in your original and natural form. I have regained my confidence and happiness. With your coming back to this sweet form I have also regained my mental balance as I was very much disturbed and in awe to see that awesome and gigantic, incredible structure.

सुदुर्दर्शमिदं रूमं दृष्टवानसि यन्मम ।
देवा अप्यस्य रूपंस्य नित्यं दर्शनकाङ्क्षिणः ॥ (XI-52) ॥

Lord Krishna says, O Arjun this form (divine) which you have seen is very rare for the ordinary people to witness. Even gods with so much of worship and holy work have not been able to see this.

नाहं वेदैर्न तपसा न दानेन न चेज्यया ।
शक्य एवंविधोद्रष्टुं दृष्टवानसि मां यथा ॥ (XI-53) ॥

O Arjun you were able to watch this unbearable spectacle but no other ordinary person could have the strength to see or bear this. This must have been due to the studies of Vedas done by you that you could have the strength and courage to see this divine form of mine.

भक्त्यात्वनन्यया शक्य अहमेवंविधोऽर्जुन ।
ज्ञातुं द्रष्टुं च तत्त्वेन प्रवेष्टुं च परंतप ॥ (XI-54) ॥

O Arjun only with prolong worship devotion and strong determination one can see this form which is very rare.

मत्कर्मकृन्मत्परमो मद्‌भक्तः संगवर्जित ।
निर्वैरः सर्वभूतेषु यः स मामेति पाण्डव ॥ (XI-55) ॥

I am always near my devotee who is selfless, full of love for Me, have devotion and urge to see Me. I am also eager to meet and see him. The person who is truthful helping the humanity, detached from all the worldly trapping *i.e.*, lust, anger, greed, attachment, ego, jealousy etc. is dear to me and my presence will always be reflected in them. I will never betray my devotee and he will find me, near him at the time of difficulty and need.

In other words, the Lord promises that He is always with pious devotees and they should not have any doubt in this.

CHAPTER XII

Lord Krishna is Explaining to Arjun about Worship and How to Perform the Same in the Right Way

एवं सततयुक्ता ये भक्तास्त्वां पर्युपासते ।
ये चाप्यक्षरमव्यक्तं तेषां के योगवित्तमाः ।। (XII-1) ।।

Arjun asks "O Lord some of your devotees worship God by placing any image or idol in front of them. And some devotees worship without the same who are following the correct way? Please let me know which of the two is the right that leads to God and salvation?

मय्यावेश्य मनो ये मां नित्ययुक्ता उपासते ।
श्रद्धया परयोपेतास्ते मे युक्ततमा मताः ।। (XII-2) ।।

O Arjun it is immaterial by which way any devotee worships *i.e.*, with the object or without it, both do not matter. It is the faith, love and belief of the devotee which matters. If a person loves Me, remembers Me with a pure heart, loves the mankind, does not harm anyone, have faith and confidence in Me then the type of worship does not matters at all. As many roads lead to the same destination, similarly the type in which to worship, does not matter.

All roads lead to the same *i.e.*, God.

येत्वक्षरमनिर्देश्चमव्यक्तं पर्युपासते ।
सर्वत्रगमचिन्त्यं च कूटस्थमचलं ध्रुवम ।। (XII-3) ।।
संनियम्येन्द्रियग्रामं सर्वत्र समबुद्धयः ।
ते प्राप्नुवन्ति मामेव सर्वभूतहिते रताः ।। (XII-4) ।।

It is immaterial whether one worships Me by placing an idol in front of him or otherwise. Both are equal so far as the objective is the same. The important thing is that the worship is with pious heart and mind having faith in the Almighty. The God is omnipotent, omnipresent and omniscient. A devotee who has faith and determination reaches Him. The forms of worship can be different, but the objective of both is to reach God.

क्लेशोऽधिकतरस्तेषा मव्यकतासक्तचेतसाम् ।

अव्यक्ता हि गतिर्दुःखं देहवम्दिरवाप्यते ॥ (XII-5) ॥

But those who worship Me in the formless body have to put more efforts to reach Me, because in this case the concentration of mind is very difficult therefore the devotee has to work harder to attain Me.

ये तु सर्वाणि कर्माणि मयि सन्यस्य मत्पराः ।

अनन्येनैव योगेन मां ध्यायन्त उपासते ॥ (XII-6) ॥

The devotee who has complete faith in God and worships with heart and soul, with pious mind and intentions is sure to reach. Him sooner or later. Only he should have faith in the Almighty. The form of worship does not matter at all. It is better to have an object (idol) before in the initial stages because one can concentrate fully.

तेषामहं समुद्धर्ता मृत्युसंसारसागरात् ।

भावामि नचिरात्पार्थ मय्यावेशितचेतसाम् ॥ (XII-7) ॥

As such who desires Me with heart and soul I definitely come and free him from all sorrows and difficulties. My devotee frees himself from all the crutches of life and attains peace of mind.

मय्येवमन आधत्स्व मयि बुद्धिं निवेशय ।

निवासिष्यसि मय्येव अत ऊर्ध्वं न संशयः ॥ (XII-8) ॥

O Arjun put all your thoughts towards Me and you will get salvation, peace of mind and you will liberate yourself from all evils and reach God.

It is very difficult to attain God but with regular practice one can reach the goal. The Lord does not mean that twenty four hours practice is needed to attain God. Let it be at the convenience of the devotee. Even for five minutes daily we can do so the same with pure mind and thought. It will take its time but in the final the devotee reaches the destination where he has to reach.

अथचिंत समाधातुं न शन्कोषि मयि स्थिरम् ।

अभ्यासयोगेन ततो मानिच्छाप्तुं धनंजय ॥ (XII-9) ॥

O Dhananjay (Arjun) with regular practice and hard work you will attain Me. Yoga, and reading of scriptures are also extremely helpful to attain this goal. Regular worship gives positive results.

अभ्यासेऽप्यसमर्थोऽसि मत्कर्मपरमो भव ।

मदर्थमपि कर्माणि कुर्वन्सिद्धिमवाप्स्यसि ॥ (XII-10) ॥

And if at all you can not do the above then you can surrender your Karmas (deeds) to Me. Even that will be enough to attain salvation in life. I will reward you for the work you have done (to the mankind) and grant you peace and happiness.

अथैतदप्य शक्तोऽसि कर्तुं मद्योगमाश्रितः ।

सर्वकर्मफलत्यांग ततः कुरू यतात्मवान् ॥ (XII-11) ॥

O Arjun even good work to the mankind and society is also equal to the worship of God. A good and pious work done by an individual never goes wasted, it is as good as worship of God. You surrender all of these Karma to Me and I will grant salvation.

Here I am reminded of a story of two friends who were going to Haridwar to have a dip in the river Ganges. On the way they reach a village where lots of people were suffering due to floods. One said to other "Let us stop here and help these suffering people." The other was against this idea. He continued the journey and the second remained in the village to help the needy persons. The friend who continued his journey had a dip in the river and went to a temple. To his utter surprise he found his friend standing behind the idol of God, but due to heavy rush could not reach him and lost in the crowd. He started his return journey and when he reached the same very village he found his friend busy in his work helping the needy people and mitigating their distress. He immediately went to him and asked as to how he could return earlier? To his utter surprise the friend told him that he was all the time in that village and did not go anywhere. Therefore doing good and pious work is also equivalent to the worship of God. God is equally aware of the good deeds done by us in this world and keeps all the account of the same.

श्रेयो हि ज्ञानमंभ्यासाज्ज्ञानाद्ध्यानं विशिष्यते ।
ध्यानात्कर्मफल त्यागस्त्यागाच्छान्तिरनन्तरम् ॥ (XII-12) ॥

Doing good work and not expecting anything in return is also a kind of Sadhana (worship) towards God. After doing service to mankind one should not expect anything in return. This is also as good as doing worship. If we can remember God from time to time, is good for the self and soul. If due to any reason it is not possible then doing service to others without any expectation is also equally rewarding and gives peace and satisfaction to a person *i.e.*, Mokshya in the end.

अद्वेष्टा सर्व भूतानां मैत्रः करूण एव च ।
निर्ममो निरहंकारः समदुःख सुखः क्षमी ॥ (XII-13) ॥

Thus a person attains peace of mind and stability in life. Such a devotee does not have any ill will against anyone, not even towards his enemies. Happiness and unhappiness do not have any effect on him. He is in calm and peaceful state of mind.

सन्तुष्टः संतत योगी यतात्मा दृढनिश्चय ।
मय्यर्पितमनोबुद्धिर्यो मभ्दक्तः स मे प्रियः ॥ (XII-14) ॥

O Arjun says Krishna, A devotee who has surrendered his ego and searches Me with a determined heart, soul and mind is sure to attain Me (God). I have a special liking for such devotees and never let them down in life.

यस्मान्नोद्विजते लोको लोकान्नोद्विजते च यः ।
हर्षामर्षभयोद्वेगैर्मुक्तो यः स च मे प्रियः ॥ (XII-15) ॥

My devotee does not harm anyone, he remains cheerful in happiness or unhappiness. He has a stable mind, performs all his duties in a happy frame of mind. He does not have any ego of any type. Such a devotee is dear to Me and remains with me at all times.

अनपेक्षः शुचिर्दक्ष उदासीनो गतव्यथः ।
सर्वारम्भपरित्यागी यो मभ्दक्तः स मे प्रियः ॥ (XII-16) ॥

A devotee who does not have high ego has no enemies. He is wise and intelligent, is not influenced by the ups and downs of life, remain calm and peaceful, has positive state of mind, has the spirit of sacrifice, and a balanced state of mind. I am always near such a devotee and he remains near my heart always.

यो न हृष्यति न द्वेष्टि न शोचति न कांक्षति ।
शुभाशुभपरित्यागी भक्तिमान्य: स मे प्रिय: ॥ (XII-17) ॥
समः शत्रौ च मित्रे च तथा मानापमानयोः ।
शीतोष्णसुखदु:खेषु समः संगविवर्जित ॥ (XII-18) ॥

My devotee is above joy and sorrow. He does not have any jealousy or enmity in him. He is away from negative tendencies and remain balanced in his life. He remains calm in adversity and does not over react in happy days. I love such a devotee of mine.

तुल्यनिन्दास्तुतिर्मौनी संतुष्टो येन केनचित् ।
अनिकेत: स्थिरमतिर्भक्तिमान्मे प्रियो नर: ॥ (XII-19) ॥

O Arjun My devotee remains satisfied. Both friends and enemies are equal in his eyes. He does not care for honour or dishonour. He is free from all the attachments of life. Has full control on desires. I (God) love such a devotee of mine.

It is easy to visualize the above but in actual practice is very difficult. But a person who is able to achieve this, he attains the power supreme and gets complete peace of mind and ultimately Mokshya *i.e.*, complete salvation in life.

ये तु धर्म्यामृतमिंद यथोक्तं पर्युपासते ।
श्रद्धधाना मत्परमा भक्तास्तेऽतीव मे प्रिया: ॥ (XII-20) ॥

O Arjun the devotee who has these qualities, is my real follower and I have great affection for him. Due to these qualities he attains peace and happiness in life. He is able to control the negative tendencies of lust, anger, greed, attachment, ego or pride and jealousy and attains Mokshya.

CHAPTER XIII

The Lord is Explaining about the Nature and Soul and Their Relationship with a Person Whereas the Body of a Person Gets Destroyed with the time but the Soul is Eternal and is Indestructible

इदं शरीरं कौन्तेय क्षेत्रमित्यभिधीयते ।

एतद्यो वेत्ति तं प्राहुः क्षेत्रज्ञ इति तद्विदः ॥ (XIII-1) ॥

Lord Krishna says, O Kaunteya (Son of Kunti), this body is the field and we sow the seeds of good thoughts, actions and deeds (Karmas) in it, as a farmer sows seeds in the field. If the seeds are rotten, the crop is also poor or bad similarly if the thoughts and actions are good we get peace and transquillity in life otherwise the harvest is unhappiness and sufferings. So it depends upon the individual whether he wants to harvest happiness and peace or the opposite.

क्षेत्रज्ञं चापि मां विद्धि सर्वक्षेत्रेषु भारत ।

क्षेत्रक्षेत्रज्ञयोर्ज्ञानं यत्तज्ज्ञानं मतं मम ॥ (XIII-2) ॥

तत्क्षेत्रं यच्च यादृक्च यद्विकारि यतश्च यत् ।

स च यो यत्प्रभावश्च तत्समासेन मे श्रृणु ॥ (XIII-3) ॥

O Arjun God is the master of the field (Soul). The knowledge is to understand the relationship of this field (Soul) and its master (God). I will explain to you about this relationship and the qualities which are needed to attain the same.

ऋषिभिर्बहुधा गीतं छन्दोभिर्विविधैः पृथक् ।

ब्रह्मसूत्रपदैश्चैव हेतुमभ्दिर्विनिश्चितै ॥ (XIII-4) ॥

महाभूतान्यंहकारो बुद्धिरव्यक्तमेव च ।

इन्द्रियाणि दशैकं च पंच चेन्द्रियगोचराः ॥ (XIII-5) ॥

इच्छाद्वेष सुखं दुःखं संघातश्चेतना धृतिः ।

एतत्क्षेत्रं समासेन सविकारमुदाहृतम् ॥ (XIII-6) ॥

The sages have also tried to explain about the relationship between the soul (body) and the master (God) in verses. The main hindrance is due to the negative factors prevailing in a person. The five basic elements *i.e.* Earth, Fire, Space, Air and Water, ten sensory organs, five sensory objects *i.e.*, sight, smell, tongue, speech and touch, etc. these cloud the soul and do not allow the soul to unite with the master (God).

When a person is able to control over these obstacles only then can he reach the master *i.e.*, God, to receive the real knowledge about the soul and the God.

अमानित्वमदम्भित्वमहिंसा क्षान्तिरार्जवम् ।

आचार्योपासनं शोचं स्थैर्यमात्मविनिग्रहः ।। (XIII-7) ।।

इन्द्रियार्थेषु वैराग्यमनहंकार एव च ।

जन्ममृत्यु जराव्याधि दुःखदोषानुदर्शनम् ।। (XIII-8) ।।

The person should not have arrogance and should not torment or harm others. Have forgiveness trait in him, should have purity of mind and body. He should have control over temptations in the world. He should not be pleasure seeker and should not have any fear of life and death in him. The fear of death hampers and a person is unable to do anything positive. He should remember that death comes once only and is sure to come to all then why to have the fear of the same.

असक्तिरनभिष्वंगः पुत्रदारगृहादिषु ।

नित्यं च समचित्तत्वमिष्टानिष्टोपपत्तिषु ।। (XIII-9) ।।

मयि चानन्ययोगेन भक्तिरव्य भिचारिणी ।

विविक्तदेशसेवित्वमरतिजर्नसंसदि ।। (XIII-10) ।।

The devotee should not have attachments *i.e.*, wife, sons, family, home or wealth etc. He should be equidistant from pleasant and unpleasant things. He should remember God, has clean thoughts, leads pious and truthful life and should not have the company of evil persons.

Though practically it is not possible in actual life but one can work for the same and whatever is achieved is sufficient for a person. Because when one comes in this world he is bound to be attracted by them, but to keep them to the minimum is helpful. The Lord further says to Arjun that the God has created this universe and the people get trapped in the Maya of arrivals and departures. This has been going on from time immemorial and will go on as the same is the creation of Almighty.

अध्यात्मज्ञानंनित्यत्वं तत्त्वज्ञानार्थं दर्शनम् ।
एतज्ज्ञानमिति प्रोक्तमज्ञानं यदतोऽन्यथा ॥ (XIII-11) ॥
ज्ञेयं यत्तत्प्रवक्ष्यामि यज्ज्ञात्वा मृतमश्नुते ।
अनादिमत्परं ब्रह्म न सत्तन्नासदुच्यते ॥ (XIII-12) ॥

O Arjun the spiritual knowledge is very important and to gain that the devotee must endeavour for the same. Doing your daily routine and doing all the same with purity of mind and heart is very essential. Gaining the knowledge from pure and positive sources, and believing in the supreme authority (God) having total faith in Him. So the knowledge thus gained or obtained is healthy and pure.

सर्वतः पाणिपादं तत्सर्वतोऽशिशिरोमुखम ।
सर्वतः श्रुतिमल्लोके सर्वमावृत्य तिष्ठति ॥ (XIII-13) ॥
सर्वेन्द्रियगुणाभांस सर्वेन्द्रियविवर्जितम ।
असक्तंसर्वभृच्चैव निगुणं गुणभोक्तृ च ॥ (XIII-14) ॥

The Brahma (God) is all around us in the universe, in arms, ears, eyes, mouths and feet. The God is devoid of senses, but at the same time is provider of all these to the mankind. The God is unattached and omnipresent and the creator as well as provider of this world. The Almighty does not have any beginning or end but eternal.

बहिरन्तश्च भूतानामंचर चरमेव च ।
सूक्ष्मत्वात्त दविज्ञेयं दूरस्थं चान्तिके च तत् ॥ (XIII-15) ॥

God is living in all the creatures on this earth. All the creations are by Him. He is so near to us at the same time very far away as well. In short, He is present in all the activities in the universe. He is near to them who remember Him and far off to those who do not do so. His presence is felt everywhere throughout the universe.

अविभक्तं च भूतेषु विभक्तमिव च स्थितम् ।
भूतभर्तृ च तज्ज्ञेयं ग्रसिष्णु प्रभविष्णु च ॥ (XIII-16) ॥

God is supposed to be indivisable but still He splits and reside in every individual be it the minutest of all the creatures. He is all powerful and present everywhere, as Vishnu the provider, as Shiva, the destroyer and as Brahma the creator in the whole universe.

ज्योतिषामपि तज्ज्योतिस्तमसः परमुच्यते ।
ज्ञानं ज्ञेयं ज्ञानगम्यं हृदि सर्वस्य विष्ठतम् ॥ (XIII-17) ॥

O Arjun God is the eternal light. He resides in every body. He is the knowledge himself but to understand Him a person requires the spiritual knowledge to reach Him.

इति क्षेत्रं तथा ज्ञानं ज्ञेयं चोक्तं समासतः ।
मद्भक्तँ एतद्विज्ञाय मदभावायोपपद्यते ॥ (XIII-18) ॥

Lord Krishna says, O Arjun I have given you this knowledge with the help of this you can attain the power to reach God. Knowledge and faith are must to attain Him, because it lights up the path in the right direction.

प्रकृति पुरूषं चैव विध्दयनादी उभावपि ।
विकाराश्च गुणांश्चैव विद्धि प्रकृतिसम्भवान् ॥ (XIII-19) ॥

Nature and soul are both without any beginning or end. They are the continuous process and happening from the time immemorial and keep on going to infinity. Attraction and repulsion are the parts of this nature as well.

कार्यकारणकर्तृत्वे हेतुः प्रकृतिरूच्यते ।
पुरूष सुखदुःखानां भोक्तृत्वे हेतुरूच्यते ॥ (XIII-20) ॥

The nature consists of body and soul. It is present throughout the universe whether in micro organism or in macro organism. The body is on this earth to enjoy happiness or pain as the case may be.

पुरूष प्रकृतिस्थो हि भुंक्ते प्रकृतिजान्गुणान् ।
कारणं गुणसगोऽस्य सदसद्योनिजन्मसु ।। (XIII-21) ।।
उपद्रष्टानुमन्ता च भर्ता भोक्ता महेश्वरः ।
परमात्मेति चाप्युक्तो देहेऽस्मिन्पुरूषः परः ।। (XIII-22) ।।

There is a strong inter-relationship between body and soul. Due to this coexistence the soul comes to this earth and the cycle of birth and death keeps on repeating in the world. The soul in the body is supreme and it is the master of the body and reflection of God.

य एवं वेत्ति पुरूषं प्रकृतिं च गुणैः सह ।
सर्वथा वर्तमानोऽपि न स भूयोऽभिजायते ।। (XIII-23) ।।
ध्यानेनात्मनि पश्यन्ति केचिदात्मानमात्मना ।
अन्ये सांख्येन योगेन कर्मयोगेन चापेर ।। (XIII-24) ।।

One who fully understands both the aspects of nature and the body, there relation to each other thus finds himself liberated from the cycle of birth and death. God is seen by many with pure mind and hearts and by many through wisdom or Gyan Yoga. The end result of the both is the same *i.e.*, Mokshya or salvation. Both are close to God whether it is through Gyan Yoga or the Karam Yoga.

अन्येत्वेवमजानन्तः श्रुत्वान्येभ्य उपासते ।
तेऽपि चातितरन्त्येव मृत्युं श्रुतिपरायणाः ।। (XIII-25) ।।
यावत्संजायते किंचित्ससत्त्वं स्थावरजंगमम् ।
क्षेत्रक्षेत्रज्ञ संयोगात्तद्विद्धि भरतर्षभ ।। (XIII-26) ।।

O Arjun who cannot understand the relationship between nature and soul can get the benefit by listening to sages and saints on this subject. O Arjun all the creatures on this earth are due to the union of nature and soul. This is the unique truth. A person who understands this finds himself liberated from the worldly attractions and negative tendencies of lust, anger, greed, attachment, ego, jealousy etc. and finally gets salvation.

समं सर्वेषु भूतेषु तिष्ठन्तं परमेश्वरम् ।

विनश्यत्स्वविनश्यन्तं यः पश्यति स पश्यति ॥ (XIII-27) ॥

समं पश्यन्हि सर्वत्र समवस्थितमीश्वरम् ।

न हिनस्त्यात्मना त्मानं ततो याति परां गतिम् ॥ (XIII-28) ॥

A person who sees God's presence in every creation whether it is small or big, good or bad, has in the real sense understood the soul knowledge. Because by this he sees the immortality of the soul and thus unites with the Almighty. The soul is indestructible neither it is born nor it dies. It is in a regular process of life and death.

प्रकृत्यैव च कर्माणि क्रियमाणानि सर्वशः ।

यः पश्यति तथात्मानमकर्तारं स पश्यति ॥ (XIII-29) ॥

यदा भूतपृथग्भावमे कस्थमनुपश्यति ।

तत एव च विस्तारं ब्रह्म सम्पद्यते तदा ॥ (XIII-30) ॥

When a person understands that whatever is happening around is by nature (God) and by the soul. He is able to understand and accept the truth of this world when he sees all the creations made by the supreme power and the individual has no part to play in the same, this is the point the devotee achieves salvation or Mokshya. He attains the truth and attains God.

अनादित्वान्निर्गुणत्वात्परमात्मायमव्ययः ।

शरीरस्थोऽपि कौन्तेय न करोति न लिप्यते ॥ (XIII-31) ॥

यथा सर्वगतं सौक्ष्म्यादाकाशं नोपलिप्यते ।

सर्वत्रा वस्थितो देहे तथात्मा नोपलिप्यते ॥ (XIII-32) ॥

O Arjun when a person feels that God is present everywhere throughout the universe, all the forces are being controlled by Him, all are the creations of God, at this stage he gets salvation *i.e.*, the complete bliss. He understands that god does not have any shape or form, has no beginning or end, lives in every creation as soul. At this stage a person becomes divine and reaches complete salvation *i.e.*, happiness and contentment.

यथा प्रकाशयत्येकः कृत्स्नं लोकमिमं रविः ।

क्षेत्रं शेत्री तथा कृत्स्नं प्रकाशयति भारत ।। (XIII-33) ।।

The Sun lights up all the other planets with its light. One Sun is able to enlight the whole world, in the same way a single pure and pious soul is able to enlight all others around him.

क्षेत्रक्षेत्रज्ञयोरेवमन्तरं ज्ञानचक्षुषा ।

भूतप्रकृतिमोक्षं च ये विदुर्यान्ति ते परम् ।। (XIII-34) ।।

Therefore a person who has understood the relationship between nature (God) and soul (body) attains the spiritual knowledge in the true sense. He is blessed with complete salvation *i.e.*, Mokshya. He can be compared with the Sun that illuminates everything around with his grace and spiritual power. He is free of all negative tendencies *i.e.*, lust, anger, greed, attachment, ego, jealousy etc. and frees himself farm all bondages of this life.

CHAPTER XIV

Here the Lord is Explaining about Knowledge (Gyan) and the Tendencies in the Individual i.e. Satvas Rajas and Tamas

परं भूयः प्रवक्ष्यामि ज्ञानानां ज्ञानमुत्तमम् ।
यज्ज्ञात्वा मुनयः सर्वे परां सिद्धिमितो गताः ॥ (XIV-1) ॥

Krishna says, O Arjun I will tell you more about knowledge through which many saints and sages have attained the ultimate (God). With this knowledge you will be able to come out from the cycle of births and deaths and finally attain peace of mind.

Though these words are being spoken by Lord Krishna to Arjun, but in reality the same is being addressed to the entire mankind to understand the same and get benefitted.

इदं ज्ञानमुपाश्रित्य मम साधर्म्यमागताः ।
सर्गेऽपि नोपजायन्ते प्रलये न व्यथन्ति च ॥ (XIV-2) ॥

O Arjun, a person who attains this knowledge frees himself from the continuous cycle of births and deaths. The person does not have any fear of the dooms day (when the world will destroy) at all because he finds himself attached with the Almighty and free from all worries and difficulties.

मम योनिर्महद्ब्रह्म तस्मिन्गर्भं दधाम्यहम्।
संभवः सर्वभूतानां ततो भवति भारत ॥ (XIV-3) ॥
सर्वयोनिषु कौन्तेय मूर्तयः सम्भवन्ति याः ।
तासां ब्रह्म महद्योनिरहं बीजप्रदः पिता ॥ (XIV-4) ॥
सत्वं रजस्तम इति गुणाः प्रकृतिसम्भवा ।
निबध्नन्ति महाबाहो देहे देहिनमव्ययम् ॥ (XIV-5) ॥

O Son of Kunti (Arjun), God is the creator of this universe. He is the creator as well as the destroyer. It is due to his powers that people take birth in this world and die. There are three types of qualities or traits in the mankind. Satva (Noble), Rajas (Attach) and Tamas (Negative). These three tendencies are found in each individual. The lesser or the greater of them forms the personality of a person.

तत्र सत्त्वं निर्मलत्वात्प्रकाशकमनामयम् ।

सुखसंगेन बध्नाति ज्ञानसगेनं चानघ ।। (XIV-6) ।।

O Arjun talking about the tendencies or traits in a person, Satva is the best of all. Satva is pure and attaches itself to happiness and knowledge. This quality generates positive and pure thoughts in an individual. This keeps the person ahead of the others and an urge in him to attain the best in his life.

रजो रागात्मकं विद्धि तृष्णासगं समुभ्दवम् ।

तन्निबध्नाति कौन्तेय कर्मसगोंन देहिनम् ।। (XIV-7) ।।

O son of Kunti (Arjun) Rajas tendency takes the individual towards attachments and pleasures of life. The person enjoys life at the same time does his duties with a positive state of mind.

तमस्त्वज्ञानजं विद्धि मोहनं सर्वदेहिनाम् ।

प्रमादालस्यनिद्रोभिस्तन्निबध्नाति भारत ।। (XIV-8) ।।

Tamas denotes negative tendencies. The person is very lazy, does not do anything positive and is seeker of pleasures without doing any effort. He sees negative in all and is unhelpful in his approach towards others. In other words all the negatives are stored in him.

The sum total of these tendencies *i.e.*, Satva, Rajas and Tamas shapes the characters and personality of an individual and he behaves accordingly in the society. If he has more of Satva and Raza traits he will be positive in his approach in life and if more of Tamas he will have negative approach and unhelpful in nature.

सत्त्वं सुखे संजयति रजः कर्मणि भारत ।

ज्ञानमावृत्य तु तमः प्रसादे संजयत्युत ।। (XIV-9) ।।

Satva trait inspires peace and happiness in an individual, Raja inspires to seek pleasures and gains while Tama gives arrogance in a person, he is full of negative tendencies and always gives harm to others in every possible way.

रजस्तमश्चाभिभूय सत्त्वं भवति भारत ।

रजःसत्त्वं तमश्चैव तमः सत्त्वं रजस्तथा ॥ (XIV-10) ॥

O Bharata (Arjun) these three tendencies compete with one another in a person to reach above the other. In other words, one competes with the other to have the upperhand *i.e.*, when Satva predominates Rajas and Tamas go down and when Rajas and Tamas dominate Satva goes down. Therefore we should try to check Rajas and Tamas tendencies so that we can lead a happy and peaceful life.

We many a times come across the people with Tamas traits in our life. We should try to avoid them as far as possible to have peace and prosperity in life.

सर्वद्वारेषु देहेऽस्मिन्प्रकाश उपजायते ।

ज्ञानं यदा तदा विद्याद्विवृद्धं सत्त्वमित्युत ॥ (XIV-11) ॥

When pious feelings, consciousness and knowledge increase in a person it is the signal that the Satva elements are on the increase in him and he is leading himself towards God. Such a person is an example for others we should try to emulated him to achieve satisfaction, peace and happiness in life.

लोभः प्रवृत्तिरारम्भः कर्मणामशमः स्पृहा ।

रजस्येतानि जायन्ते विवृद्धे भरतर्षभ ॥ (XIV-12) ॥

When Rajas tendencies predominate, the feelings of pleasure come to a person, greed, selfish desires reach the peak. Strong feelings of pleasure dominate. Therefore one must try to inculcate satva tendencies to reach peace and happiness. There is constant conflict amongst Satva, Rajas and Tamas traits to dominate. A person should curb Rajas and Tamas tendencies to have a peaceful life.

अप्रकाशोऽप्रवृत्तिश्च प्रमादो मोह एव च ।

तमस्येतानि जायन्ते विवृद्धे कुरूनन्दन ॥ (XIV-13) ॥

O Kurunandan (Arjun) when the tendencies of greed, selfishness, harm, are on the rise, disinterest in pious deeds increase in a person that shows the increase of Tamas tendencies in an individual.

He should try to come out from them as no one else can help him in this. It is only his willingness and determination which can help him to come out from them.

यदा सत्त्वे प्रवृद्धे तु प्रलयं याति देहभृत् ।

तदोत्तमविदां लोकानमलान्प्रतिपद्यते ॥ (XIV-14) ॥

When a person has Satva traits or tendencies he is devoid of all the negative forces. He frees himself from the cycle of births and deaths and goes to Baikunth or the abode of the God. He attains supreme peace, happiness and the state of complete rest. He does not come back on this earth again and enjoys complete bliss of Almighty *i.e.*, Mokshya.

रजसि प्रलयं गत्वा कर्मसगिंषु जायते ।

तथा प्रलीनस्तमसि मूढयोनिषु जायते ॥ (XIV-15) ॥

The person who has Rajas tendencies is reborn in a wealthy and renowned family and once again undergoes the cycle of birth and death till he gets salvation through Satva Karmas. But the person with Tamas traits keep on coming and going. He has to undergo so many hardships again and again.

कर्मण सुकृतस्याहुः सात्त्विकं निर्मलं फलम् ।

रजसस्तु फलं दुखमज्ञानं तमसः फलम् ॥ (XIV-16) ॥

The persons who do Satva Karmas are rewarded by God with peace, happiness, satisfaction and salvation *i.e.*, Mokshya. The Karmas inspired by Rajas tendencies give relief from woes, but the Karmas inspired by Tamas tendencies takes one towards ignorance and evil forces. The result of the same is unhappiness, fear, worry and negative energy. The person with these traits or tendencies remain unhappy and wonders here and there, achieves nothing, neither for himself nor for the others who come in contact with him.

सत्त्वात्सं जायते ज्ञानं रजसो लोभ एव च ।

प्रमादमोहौ तमसो भवतोऽज्ञानमेव च ।। (XIV-17) ।।

The qualities of Satva trait are responsible for knowledge and wisdom in an individual. The qualities of Rajas inspire greed and want and pleasure in a person, while that of Tamas give unhappiness, ignorance and worry.

So a person should strive for the Satva qualities in himself as far as possible. It is quite difficult but with strong will one can achieve the same, as there is nothing difficult with strong will and determination.

ऊर्ध्वं गच्छन्ति सत्त्वस्था मध्ये तिष्ठन्ति राजसाः ।

जघन्यगुण वृत्तिस्था अधो गच्छन्ति तामसाः ।। (XIV-18) ।।

The person who has Satva traits gets happiness and gets complete liberation from the worldly trappings and attractions. The person with Rajas traits has to come back for sometime on this earth again before he gets salvation. But the person with Tamas traits keeps on coming and going in the world. The Satva is the noblest of the three.

नान्यं गुणेभ्यः कर्तारं यदा द्रष्टानुपश्यति ।

गुणेभ्यश्च परं वेत्ति मभ्दावं सोऽधिगच्छति ।। (XIV-19) ।।

When a person is able to understand that all the creations are equal in the eyes of God and does not discriminates with any one, he becomes enlighten. He sees the hand of Almighty in all actions and creations. At this stage he attains salvation and freedom from all the evil forces.

गुणानेतानतीत्य त्रीन्देही देहसमुभ्दवान् ।

जन्ममृत्युजरादुःखैर्विमुक्तोऽमृतमश्नुते ।। (XIV-20) ।।

Having understood thus a person reaches the stage of perfection and total bliss. He frees himself from the cycle of births and deaths and becomes immortal, the gates of heaven open to him as a token of reward by the God as he has liberated himself from the three *i.e.*, Satva, Rajas and

Tamas traits and so also the negative tendencies of Lust, Greed, Anger, Attachments, Ego, Jealousy, etc.

कैर्लिंगैस्त्रीन्गुणानेतानतीतो भवति प्रभो ।

किमाचारः कथं चैतांस्त्रीन्गुणानतिवर्तते ।। (XIV-21) ।।

Arjun says to Krishna O Lord a person who has conquered all the three tendencies, how do we recognise him? and who he is able to achieve it *i.e.* How he is able to conquer them?

प्रकाश च प्रवृतिं च मोहमेव च पाण्डव ।

न द्वेष्टि सम्प्रवृत्तानि न निवृत्तानि कांक्षति ।। (XIV-22) ।।

उदासीनवदासीनो गुणैर्यो न विचाल्यते ।

गुणा वर्तन्त इत्येव योऽवतिष्ठति नेगंते ।। (XIV-23) ।।

समदुःखसुखः स्वस्थः समलोष्टाश्मकाचनः ।

तुल्यप्रियाप्रियो धीरस्तुल्यनिन्दात्मसंस्तुति ।। (XIV-24) ।।

O Son of Pandu (Arjun) The three tendencies *i.e.*, Satva, leads to light and knowledge, Rajas increases desires and pleasures and Tamas is responsible for the negative feelings in a person. The one who conquers them becomes pure and pious. He is uneffected by pleasure and pain, joy or sorrow and ups and downs of life. He is uneffected by all these. He behaves in a very balanced manner and away from the negative tendencies of Lust, Anger, Greed, Attachments, Ego and Jealousy, etc. A strong will and determination is required to tide over all these tendencies and the person who is able to achieve this is a Yogi. The doors of heaven open to him and he comes out of the cycle of births and deaths.

मानापमानयोस्तुल्यस्तुल्यो मित्रारिप्रक्षयोः ।

सर्वारम्भपरित्यागी गुणातीतः स उच्यते ।। (XIV-25) ।।

O Arjun says Krishna such a person has no friends or enemies, he is equidistant from both of them. He does not have any pride or ego. These are the signs of a real Yogi.

मां च योऽव्यभिचारेण भक्तियोगेन सेवते ।

स गुणान्समतीत्यैतान्ब्रह्मभूयाय कल्पते ॥ (XIV-26) ॥

One who remembers God and remains in search of truth, he gets strength to have control over all the evil forces. He is able to check the three tendencies *i.e.*, Satva, Rajas and Tamas in life.

ब्रह्मणो हि प्रतिष्ठाहममृतस्याव्ययस्य च ।

शाश्वतस्य च धर्मस्य सुखस्यैकान्तिकस्य च ॥ (XIV-27) ॥

O Arjun the names of the Almighty are many *i.e.*, Brahma, Supreme, Divine etc. You can worship any one of them because all lead to one and the same power Almighty who is the custodian of his universe.

CHAPTER XV

The Lord is Explaining about God in the Chapter. The World is Like a Tree. The Roots are the Almighty (God), the Trunk is Brahma and the Leaves are the Vedas

ऊधर्वमूलमधः शाखमश्वत्थं प्राहुरव्ययम् ।
छन्दांसि यस्य पर्णानि यस्तं वेद स वेदवित् ।। (XV-1) ।।

Krishna says O Arjun, The world is like an inverted tree. The main branch is Brahma and the leaves are the Vedas. The person who understands this has the real knowledge of Vedas. To know about the real life, the knowledge of Vedas helps a lot in that direction.

अधरचोर्ध्वं प्रसृतास्तस्य शाखा गुणप्रवृद्धा विषयप्रवालाः ।
अध्रश्च मूलान्यनुसन्ततानि कर्मानुबन्धीनि मनुष्यलोके ।। (XV-2) ।।

This world tree is watered by the three tendencies *i.e.*, Satva, Rajas and Tama. Desires and pleasures are the buds of this tree, human and the sub species are the branches, lust, pride vanity etc. are the roots. They alltogether bind the human life from all sides.

न रूपमस्येह तथोपलभ्यते नान्तो न चादिर्न च सम्प्रतिष्ठा।
अश्चवत्थमेन सुविरूढमूलं मसंगशस्त्रेण दृढेन छित्वा ।। (XV-3) ।।

This tree has taken deep roots. It is extremely difficult to understand because it does not have any beginning or the end. We can cut the roots of this tree by detachment from the worldly trappings and attractions. It is always better to trim it from time to time during the course of journey (life time) by an individual.

ततः पदं तत्परिमागिर्तव्यं
यस्मिन्गता न निवर्तन्ति भूयः ।
तमेव चाद्यं पुरूषं प्रपद्ये
यतः प्रवृत्तिः प्रसृता पुराणी ।। (XV-4) ।।

A person must remain in pursuit of the Almighty while on this earth because God is the creator as well as the destroyer of this world. We should remain totally detached and keep on doing our duties in the right earnest with positive state of mind and attitude, so as to reach the Almighty at the end of our journey.

निर्मानमोहा जितसगंदोषाः अध्यात्मनित्या विनिवृत्तकामाः ।
द्वन्द्वैर्विमुक्ताः सुखदुःख संज्ञैः गच्र्छन्त्यमूढाः पदंमव्यंय तत् ।। (XV-5) ।।

A person with the spiritual knowledge thus gained becomes desireless, selfless and away from greed, infatuations and ultimately attains Mokshya and unite with God.

न तभ्दासयते सूर्यो न शशांको न पावकः ।
यद्गत्वा न निर्वतन्ते तध्दाम परमं मम ।। (XV-6) ।।

The God is self luminous and does not require the light of the Sun, moon or fire. On the other hand He is the provider of the same to all others. The pious and spiritual person who reaches this abode of God does not come back on this earth again. He enjoys the rest of his life in the abode of the power supreme for ever.

ममैवांशो जीवलोके जीवभूतः सनातनः ।
मम षष्टानीन्द्रियाणि प्रकृतिस्थानि कर्षति ।। (XV-7) ।।

O Arjun the soul in the body is the part of God. He has provided soul to human and other living beings. The soul enters the natural self and attracts mind and the five senses of knowledge and keeps on the cycle of birth and deaths in this world.

The soul in the body can be compared with petrol in a car. So far the petrol is there the car keeps on moving and the time it is exhausted the car cannot run anymore. The only difference being that we can see and touch petrol but the soul is invisible and cannot be touched or seen.

शरीरं यदवाप्नोति यच्चाप्युत्क्रामतीश्वरः ।
गृहीत्वैतानि संयाति वायुर्गन्धानिवाशयात् ।। (XV-8) ।।

Just like a strong breaze takes away the fragrance of the flowers in the same way the soul takes away the mind and the five senses out of the body and enters the next. This keeps repeating till the person gets Mokshya or salvation.

श्रोत्रंचक्षुः स्पर्शनं च रसंन ध्राणमेव च ।
अधिष्ठाय मनश्चायं विषयानुपसेवते ।। (XV-9) ।।

The soul enjoys the pleasure of life through ears, eyes, tongue, nose and mind while living in the body of a person.

उत्क्रामन्त स्थितं वापि भुजान वा गुणान्वितम ।
विमूढा नानुपश्यन्ति पश्यन्ति ज्ञानंचक्षुष ॥ (XV-10) ॥

But the ignorant cannot understand this. He feels that the body and the soul are the same but in reality they are two different identities. Wisemen with knowledge and learning can feel the difference of the soul and the body.

यतन्तो योगिनश्चैनं पश्यन्त्यात्मन्यवस्थितम् ।
यतन्तोऽप्यकृतात्मानो नैनं पश्यन्त्यचेतसः ॥ (XV-11) ॥

A pious, wise and learned person knows that the soul is present in the heart of the body. But a person who is ignorant does not trust, cannot understand this phenomenon because his conscious is not clear.

यदादित्यगतं तेजो जगभ्दासयतेऽखिलम् ।
यच्चन्द्रमसि यच्चाग्नौ तत्तेजो विद्धि मामकम् ॥ (XV-12) ॥

The light and heat in the Sun, Moon and fire are all provided by God in them. Only God is self luminous and all the other bodies received the same from Him (God). In other words the Lord is the provider of all the energy in the universe.

There is a story about Lord Krishna and his wife Rukmani. The Lord was sitting in his Chamber, she comes to him and asks as to who provides food to everyone in this world? Krishna tells her that it is due to God. She was not convinced. She takes an insect and puts it in a small box, closes the lid and asks Krishna will God provide food to this insect? Lord replied in the positive and asks Rukmani to open it in the morning. When she opened the box she was surprised to see that the little insect was busy eating a small piece of rice. She was confused and asks Krishna as to how all this happened? The Lord smiled and said to Rukmani when she was closing the lid the little piece of rice fell from vermilion on her forehead, thus the Almighty provided food to the little creature.

गामाविश्य च भूतानि धारयाम्यहमोजसा ।
पुष्णामि चौषधीः सर्वाः सोमो भूत्वा रसात्मकः ॥ (XV-13) ॥
अहंवैश्वानरो भूत्वा प्राणिनां देहमाश्रितः ।
प्राणापानसमायुक्तः पचाम्यन्नं चतुर्विधम् ॥ (XV-14) ॥

God is the creator and sustainer of this universe. The Almighty comes on this earth with his divine powers. He is present in all the creatures in this world whether human, animals or plants. He provides food and life in all of them. He showers rays of moonlight as nectar on the plants to provide life and food to them. God is the provider of all in this universe.

सर्वस्य चाहं हृदि सन्निविष्टो मत्तः स्मृतिर्ज्ञान मपोहनं च ।
वेदैश्य सर्वैरहमेव वेद्यो वेदान्तकृद्वेदविदेव चाहम् ॥ (XV-15) ॥

God is present everywhere on this earth. He is the creator of knowledge, wisdom and memory in a person. He is the creator of this universe, the author and scholar of vedas. A person can reach him through the study of the vedas, creation of the God. They are the most ancient authority on spiritualism.

द्वाविमौ पुरूषो लोके क्षरश्चाक्षर एव च ।
क्षरः सर्वाणि भूतानि कूटस्थो ऽक्षर उच्यते ॥ (XV-16) ॥

There are two types of people on this earth. One is mortal and the other is immortal. The human being, plants, animals etc. they all are mortal bodies made of five elementary elements Fire: water, air, earth and ethereal fluid and will dissolve into these elements while the soul is immortal and is a continuous process. Fire cannot burn it, water cannot drown it and no weapon of any kind can destroy it.

उत्तमः पुरूषस्त्वन्यः परमात्मेत्युदाहृतः ।
यो लोकत्रयमा विश्य बिभर्त्य व्यय ईश्वरः ॥ (XV-17) ॥

The wisemen who understand God submit to Him with complete faith and devotion. They repose their full faith in the Almighty. It is only total devotion which brings any individual towards God. Surrender yourself to God. That is the best "support". One who knows about this support, becomes free from all fears, anxieties and sorrow.

यस्मात्क्षरमती तोऽहमक्षरादपि चोत्तमः ।

अतोऽस्मि लोके वेदे च प्रथितः पुरूषोत्तमः ।। (XV-18) ।।

God is superior and completely different from the mortal body. That is why he is known as power supreme or Parmatma. He is all powerful, present everywhere, driving the wheels of this universe. It is due to him people come on this earth, after completing their duties return to the other state as per their Karmas (deeds).

यो मामेवमसंमूढो जानाति पुरूषोत्तमम् ।
स सर्वविभ्दजति मां सर्वभावेन भारत ।। (XV-19) ।।
इति गुह्यंतमशास्त्रमिदमुक्तं मयानध ।
एतद् बुद्ध्वा बुद्धिमान्स्यात्कृतकृत्यश्च भारत ।। (XV-20) ।।

O Arjun wise and learned men have complete confidence in God. Lord Krishna says to Arjun, I revealed to you about this spiritual knowledge, who understands this is a perfect man and is like a sage or saint. With this knowledge a person can purify himself and this is the path to reach the power supreme. With pure tendencies of self-less work and sinceare effort a person can reach his goal *i.e.*, understanding God, the nature and soul, there relationship with one another and can free himself from the cycle of births and deaths and attain Mokshya or the ultimate bliss.

CHAPTER XVI

Krishna is Explaining about Holy Individuals and the Evil Minded Persons. The Pious and Holy Persons are Always Positive in their Approach While the Wvil Persons always see the Negative side of all Such Things

अभयं सत्वसंशुद्धिर्ज्ञानयोगव्यवस्थितिः।
दानं दमश्च यज्ञश्च स्वाध्यायस्तप आर्जवम् ॥ (XVI-1) ॥

Krishna says, O Arjun I will tell you about the holy individuals and evil minded ones. The person who has clear conscious, have spiritual bend of mind; charitable nature, having control over senses, having simple mind and habits, has Satva traits. Such a person is a holy person and he who is devoid of these is an evil one. Fearless and straight forward, does self-less work worshipper of God has Satva traits. Such person is a holy person and he who is devoid of these is an evil one.

अहिंसा सत्यमक्रोधस्त्यागः शान्तिरपैशुनम् ।
दया भूतेष्वलोलुप्त्वं मार्दवं ह्रोरचापलम् ॥ (XVI-2) ॥

A holy person believes in peace. He does not hurt anyone physically or with spoken words, he is truthful and calm, has no ill will against anyone but at the same time truly compassionate and is not slave of desires of helpful nature and loves the mankind.

तेजः क्षमा धृतिः शौचमद्रोहो नातिमानिता ।
भवन्ति समपदं दैवाम-भिजातस्य भारत ॥ (XVI-3) ॥

O Arjun a holy person has the qualities of intelligence, forgiveness, patience, purity of mind and is without any ego or arrogance. With these positive qualities he is always near the Almighty and his life is full of happiness and contentment. He is eager to help others in need and always busy in positive deeds.

दम्भोदर्योअभिमानश्च क्रोधः पारूष्यमेवं च ।
अज्ञानं चाभिजातस्य पार्थ सम्पदमासुरीम् ॥ (XVI-4) ॥

O Parth (Arjun) on the other hand the evil minded persons show the signs of arrogance are full of ego, short tempered, boastful, harsh and ignorant. They see only the negative side of any situation. Eager to fight and are of quarrel some nature, full of anger. They get pleasure in harming others. For their little gain they are always ready to harm the others. These are the signs of an evil minded persons.

दैवी सम्पद्विमोक्षाय निबन्धायासुरी मता ।

माशुचः सम्पंद दैवी मभिजातोऽसि पाण्डवः ।। (XVI-5) ।।

O Arjun the pious traits give satisfaction and happiness in life while the evil ones lead towards unhappiness, ignorance and negative tendencies. Arjun you should not worry about this because you are pious and have positive tendencies in you. As such you need not worry as you are full of divine qualities.

द्वौ भूतसर्गौ लोकेऽस्मिन्दैव आसुर एव च ।

दैवो विस्तरशः प्रोक्त आसुरं पार्थ मे श्रृणु ।। (XVI-6) ।।

The evil minded persons always indulge in negative deeds. They harm all who come in contact with them. They are full of negative energy and thoughts *i.e.*, Lust, Anger, Greed, Attachments, Ego, Jealousy, etc.

प्रवृति च निवृति च जना न विदुरासुराः ।

न शौचं नप्पि चाचारो न सत्यं तेषु विद्यते ।। (XVI-7) ।।

The evil minded are untruthful, they will always harm others and cannot be trusted because they can harm any time. They are boastful in nature and see only the negative side.

असंत्यमप्रतिष्ठं ते जगदाहुरनीश्वरम् ।

अप्रस्परसम्भूंत किमन्यत्कामहैतुकम ।। (XVI-8) ।।

They (evil minded) feel that the God has nothing to do with the nature and has no role to play in this world. The universe has come into being of its own and God has no role in its making. In other words they see only the negative side.

एतां दृष्टिमवष्टभ्य नष्टात्मानोऽल्पबुद्धयः ।

प्रभवन्त्युग्रकर्माणः क्षयाय जगतोऽहिताः ॥ (XVI-9) ॥

People of such character are bound to harm others, the nature and the world as well. Due to their negative energy they only spread gloom and uncertainty. They do not believe in the Almighty. Such persons are ignorant and see only the dark side of the picture.

काममाश्रित्य दुष्पूरं दम्भमानमदान्विताः ।

मोहाद्गृहीत्वासद्ग्राहान्प्रवर्तन्तेऽशुचिव्रताः ॥ (XVI-10) ॥

Such type of persons keep on coming and going in this world. They never get salvation and keep on roaming endless without any aim or goal in their lives.

चिन्तामपरिमेयां च प्रलयान्तामुपाश्रिताः ।

कामोपभोगपरमा एतावदिति निश्चिताः ॥ (XVI-11) ॥

Till the end they are engrossed in worries and anxieties. They are unable to do any productive or worthwhile job in this world. The evil minded persons are always busy accumulating wealth with wrong and evil actions and cannot come out from the cycle of births and deaths.

आशापाशशतैर्बद्धा कामक्रोधपरायणाः ।

ईहन्ते कामभोगार्थमन्यायेनार्थसंचयान् ॥ (XVI-12) ॥

The person with negative tendencies become prisoner of Lust, Anger, Greed, Attachment, Ego, Jealousy, etc. and cannot come out of them. With amassing more and more wealth he cannot see any other positive side of his existence. In short he becomes prisoner of his own actions and cannot get spiritual happiness or salvation in life.

इदमद्य मया लब्धमिमं प्राप्स्ये मनोरथम् ।

इदमस्तीदमपि मे भविष्यति पुनर्धनम् ॥ (XVI-13) ॥

Such type of persons are only busy is amassing wealth and think that their mission on this earth is to get wealth and pleasures. This lust for material pleasures never subsides in them.

असौ मया हतः शत्रुर्हनिष्ये चापरानपि ।

ईश्वरोऽहमहं भोगी सिद्धोऽहं बलवान्सुखी ।। (XVI-14) ।।

In the process of amassing wealth they create many enemies for themselves. Sometime, they kill someone or get killed by others in the process. This keeps on going in their cases till the end.

आढयोऽभिजनवानस्मिकोऽन्योऽस्ति सदृशो मया ।

यक्ष्ये दास्यामि मोदिष्य इत्यज्ञानविमोहिताः ।। (XVI-15) ।।

अनेकचित्तविभ्रान्ता मोहजालसमावृताः ।

प्रसक्ताः कामभोगेषु पतन्ति नरकेऽशुचौ ।। (XVI-16) ।।

The excess of wealth and power put them on the wrong path. They feel that no one other is stronger than them. With these attachments they keep on falling deeper and deeper and are unable to recover from this trap.

आत्मसम्भाविताः स्तब्धा धनमानमदान्विताः ।

यजन्ते नामयज्ञैस्ते दम्भेनाविधिपूर्वकम् ।। (XVI-17) ।।

अहंकारं बलं दर्पं कामं क्रोधं च सांश्रेताः ।

मामात्मपरदेहेषु प्राद्विषन्तोऽभ्यसूयकाः ।। (XVI-18) ।।

The abundance of wealth and pleasures, power and honour corrupt these people. In the lust of greed, anger, pride, etc. they harm others. They feel that they are the strongest on this earth. But they do not understand that God resides in the hearts of the other persons as well and thus they make God as their enemy in the process.

तानहं द्विषतः क्रूरान्संसारेषु नराधमान् ।

क्षिपाम्यजस्त्रमशुभानासुरीष्वेव योनिषु ।। (XVI-19) ।।

आसुंरी योनिमापन्ना मूढा जन्मनि जन्मनि ।

मामप्राप्यैव कौन्तेय ततो यान्त्यधमां गतिम् ।। (XVI-20) ।।

O Son of Kunti (Arjun), the evil persons are sent to hell by the Almighty and they have to undergo many confinements. They are unable to come out the cycle of births and deaths and keep on coming and going without salvation.

त्रिविंध नरकस्येदं द्वारं नाशनमात्मनः ।

कामः क्रोधस्तथा लोभस्तस्मादेतत्त्रयं त्यजेत् ॥ (XVI-21) ॥

O Arjun, Lust, Anger and Greed are the gates of hell. We should try to discard them from our lives as far as possible. With these tendencies a person cannot do anything good in the society and is unable to attain his goal.

एतैर्विमुक्तः कौन्तेय तमोद्वारै स्त्रिभिर्नरः ।

आचरन्त्यात्मन श्रेयस्ततो याति परां गतिम् ॥ (XVI-22) ॥

A person is able to free himself from the above three tendencies if an honest effective steps are taken in that direction by him.

यः शास्त्रविधिमुत्सृज्य वर्तते कामकारतः ।

न स सिद्धिमवाप्नोति न सखं न परां गतिम् ॥ (XVI-23) ॥

A person who has freed himself from the three doors of hell *i.e.*, Lust, Anger, Greed and makes an honest effort can definitely reach God. But those who do not believe in the holy books and scriptures lead miserable lives and wonder here and there without happiness or contentment in their lives. Such persons can be compared with those who are lost in a deep forest and are unable to find any way out of the same. They keep on moving lost in the forest and are unable to reach the final destination.

तस्माच्छास्त्रं प्रमाणं ते कार्याकार्यव्यवस्थितौ ।

ज्ञात्वा शास्त्रविधानोक्तं कर्म कर्तुमिहार्हसि ॥ (XVI-24) ॥

Krishna says, O Arjun you must make up your mind in accordance with the guidelines given in the scriptures and other holy books about the war against the Kauravas.

[illegible]

[illegible] demons. They are unable to come out of the cycle of birth and death and keep on coming and going without salvation.

[illegible]

[illegible] ॥(XVI-21)॥

O Arjun! Lust, Anger and Greed are the gates of hell. We should try to discard them from our lives as far as possible. With these tendencies a person cannot do anything good in the world and is unable to attain his goal.

[illegible]

[illegible] ॥(XVI-22)॥

A person [illegible]

[illegible]

[illegible] ॥(XVI-23)॥

[illegible]

[illegible] their tendencies are unable to find any way out [illegible] and [illegible] attain the final destination.

[illegible]

[illegible] ॥(XVI-24)॥

[illegible] Arjun, you must make up your mind in accordance with the methods given in the scriptures and other holy books about the war against the Kauravas.

CHAPTER XVII

In this chapter Krishna is explaining to Arjun about Penances (Worship), Foods, Yajnas, Charities, etc. They are of three types i.e. Satvic, Rajasic and Tamasic

ये शास्त्रविधिमुत्सृज्य यजन्ते श्रद्धान्विताः ।

तेषां निष्ठा तु का कृष्ण सत्त्वमाहो रजस्तमः ॥ (XVII-1) ॥

Arjun asks, O Krishna what will happen to those persons who worship God with full faith and according to scriptures and holy books. Please let me know the fate of such persons.

त्रिविधा भवति श्रद्धा देहिनां सा स्वभावजा ।

सात्त्विकी राजसी चैव तामसी चेति तां शृणु ॥ (XVII-2) ॥

O Arjun a person's natural faith depends upon the three fold characters or tendencies *i.e.*, Satvic, Rajasic and Tamasic. I will explain to you in details about all of them.

सत्वानुरूपा सर्वस्य श्रद्धा भवति भारत ।

श्रद्धामयोऽयं पुरूषो यो यच्छ्रद्धः स एवं सः ॥ (XVII-3) ॥

O Bharata (Arjun) a persons faith depends upon his inner nature or temperament. He is the product of what faith makes of him. The faith is very important character, without it, it is not possible to worship God. In other words faith is worship.

यजन्ते सात्त्विका देवान्यक्षरक्षांसि राजसाः ।

प्रेतान्भूतगणांश्चान्ये यजन्ते तामसा जनाः ॥ (XVII-4) ॥

The persons with Satva traits worship deities or other gods. The Rajasic persons worship Rakshas and the person with Tamasic traits worship ghosts and spirits. So from the same we can infer the nature of an individual.

अशास्त्रविहितं घोरं तप्यन्ते ये तपो जनाः ।

दम्भाहंकारसंयुक्ताः कामरागबलान्विताः ॥ (XVII-5) ॥

But O Arjun who do penance only to show off or exhibit to others their physical or spiritual power are of Sanatic nature. They do no good to themselves because that shows only ego, pride and wishful state of mind. This type of penance does not pay neither to the person who does it nor to the person who sees it.

कर्शयन्तः शरीरस्थं भूतग्राममचेतसः ।

मां चैवान्तःशरीरस्थं तान्विद्धयासुरनिश्चयान् ॥ (XVII-6) ॥

The persons who offer body, heart, sensory organs, earth, fire, water to God with their penance just to show off or attain physical powers to harm other, these are ignorant persons and are evil minded.

आहारसत्वापि सर्वस्य त्रिविधो भवति प्रियः ।

यज्ञस्तपस्तथा दानं तेषां भेदमिमं श्रृणु ॥ (XVII-7) ॥

As religious devotion is of three kinds similarly the food taken by us is also of three kinds as Yajna (Pooja), penance (Tap) and charity (daan). I will (Krishna) let you (Arjun) about them in details.

आयुः सत्त्वबलारोग्यसुख प्रितिविवर्धनाः ।

रस्याः स्निग्धाः स्थिरा हृद्या आहाराः सात्त्विक प्रियाः ॥ (XVII-8) ॥

कटवम्ललवणातयुष्णतीक्ष्ण रूक्षं विदाहिनः ।

आहारा राजसस्येष्टा दुःखशोकामयप्रदाः ॥ (XVII-9) ॥

यातयामं गतरसं पूति मर्युषितं च यत् ।

उच्छिष्ट मपि चामेध्यं भोजनं तामसप्रियम् ॥ (XVII-10) ॥

The food of Satvic persons is nourishing, healthy and easy to digest. They mostly eat fruits and other health improving foods, which keep them healthy and in good state of mind and heart.

The food of Rajasic persons is oily, salty, sour, very hot and spicy. They do not go for healthy food but take tasty food only.

The food of the Tamasic persons is stale not properly cooked, left over of yesterday. Such food is not health giving.

अफलाकांक्षिभि:यज्ञो विधिदृष्टो य इज्यते ।
यष्टव्यमेवेति मनः समाधाय स सात्त्वकः ।। (XVII-11) ।।
अभिसन्धाय तु फलं दर्म्मार्थमपि चैव यत् ।
इज्यते भरतश्रेष्ठ तं यज्ञं विद्धि राजसम् ।। (XVII-12) ।।
विधिहीनमसृष्टान्नं मंत्रहीन मदक्षिणम् ।
श्रद्धाविरहितं यज्ञं तामसं परिचक्षते ।। (XVII-13) ।।

Yajna performed with positive attitude with faith in its results and without any desire is termed as Satvic Yajna. Yajna done to impress others with ego and with selfish motive is Rajasic Yajna.

Yajna done without any faith is termed as Tamasic Yajna and does not gives any result.

देवद्विजगुरूप्राज्ञपूजनं शौचमाजर्वम् ।
ब्रह्यचर्यमहिसां च शरीरं तप उच्यते ।। (XVII-14) ।।
अनुद्वेगकर वाक्यं सत्यं प्रियाहितं च यत् ।
स्वाध्यायाभ्यसनं चैव वागंमयं तप उच्यते ।। (XVII-15) ।।
मनः प्रसादः सौम्यत्वं मौनमात्मविनिग्रहः ।
भावसंशुद्धिरित्येतत्तपो मानसमुच्यते ।। (XVII-16) ।।

O Arjun there are three types of penances (act of self mortification *i.e.*, Tap) (*a*) Physical, (*b*) Speech, (*c*) Mind.

(*a*) Respect to God, sages, teacher, parents, keeping clean, celibacy, doing Yajnas with pure and pious mind, these are the physical penances.

(*b*) Not offending any person with speech. Talking to everyone with respect and love not abusing any person. Not hurting anyone with words. These are the speech penances.

(*c*) Keeping the mind pure. Remaining happy and keeping others also happy, these are the penances of mind.

The three help a person to remain on the positive side of life away from the evil tendencies of Lust, Anger, Greed, Attachment, Ego and Jealousy, etc.

श्रद्धया परया तप्तं तपस्तत्त्रिविधं नरैः ।

अफलाकांक्षिभियुक्तैः सात्त्विंक परिचक्षते ॥ (XVII-17) ॥

O Arjun all the three penances done by a person are termed as Satvic penances (Tap).They are done by a devotee without any expectation and with a pious state of mind.

सत्कारमानपूजार्थं तपो दम्भेन चैव यत् ।

क्रियते तदिह प्रोक्त राजसं चलमध्रुवम् ॥ (XVII-18) ॥

Penance done with some expectations and reaping fruits of the same, is termed as Rajasic penance. There is some motive behind this penance as such Rajasic.

मूढग्राहेणात्मनो यत्पीडया क्रियते तपः ।

परस्योत्सादनार्थं वा तत्तामसमुदाहृतम् ॥ (XVII-19) ॥

And the penance done without any motive just to show off to others or to do harm to anybody is termed as Tamasic penance because it is done keeping negative tendencies in mind.

दातव्यमिति यद्दानं दीयतेऽनुपकारिणे ।

देशे काले च पात्रे च तद्दानं सात्विकं स्मृतम् ॥ (XVII-20) ॥

Charity done for a good cause thus helping others for a social cause is termed as Satvic. It should be done without expectation of any results or favour.

यत्तु प्रत्युपकारार्थं फलमुद्दिश्य वा पुनः ।

दीयते च परिकिल्प्टं तद्दानं राजसं स्मृतम् ॥ (XVII-21) ॥

Charity done with some motive behind or with the expectation of some results or rewards is termed as Rajasic. This charity as such is considered noble anyway, but it should be without expectation or rewards.

अदेशकाले यद्दानमपात्रेभ्यश्च दीयते ।

असत्कृतमवज्ञातं तत्तामसमुदाहृतम् ॥ (XVII-22) ॥

Charity done with ill will or in a forced manner, given to those who do not deserve or given to those knowingly that it will be misused, these all charities are termed as Tamasic.

There is no use of giving such type of charities because it is neither helpful to the giver nor who has received and there is no benefit for such charities.

ओम् तत्सदिति निर्देशो ब्रह्मणस्त्रिविधः स्मृतः ।

ब्राह्मणास्तेन वेदाश्च यज्ञाश्च विहिताः पुरा ॥ (XVII-23) ॥

'Om' 'Tat' and 'Sat' are the three symbolic letters representing the Almighty (Brahma who created this universe), Vedas and Yajnas *i.e.*, the total life support system of the whole world.

तस्मादोमित्युदाहृत्य यज्ञदान तपः क्रियाः ।

प्रवर्तन्ते विधानोक्ताः सततं ब्रह्मवादिनाम् ॥ (XVII-24) ॥

The letter 'Om' is very auspiecious. All Yajnas, charities, penances are started with 'Om' as a symbolic recitation. This word is associated with the name of Almighty and carries special significance in the Vedas and other spiritual books. 'Om' stands for God who looks after the universe.

तदित्यनभिसन्धाय फलं यज्ञतपः क्रियाः ।

दानक्रियाश्च विविधाः क्रियन्ते मो क्षकाङ्क्षिभि ॥ (XVII-25) ॥

The seekers of truth, salvation (Mokshya) and liberation perform Yajnas, penances and charities with faith in Almighty (God) and in His name *i.e.*, 'Tat' the supreme power. Thus ensure divine blessings and get liberated from the cycle of births and deaths. They do not come back and rest in the heaven after death *i.e.*, Mokshya.

सद्भवि साधुभावे च सदित्येतत्प्रयुज्यते ।

प्रशस्ते कर्मणि तथा सच्छदः पार्थ युज्यते ॥ (XVII-26) ॥

O Parth (Arjun), The word 'Sat' stands for good and truth. At the beginning of any spiritual work this word *i.e.*, 'Sat' is recited. It is also used in reference to right deeds. It is very pious word indeed.

यज्ञे तपसि दाने च स्थितिः सदिति चोच्यते ।

कर्म चैव तदर्थीय सदित्येवाभिधीयते ॥ (XVII-27) ॥

All the Yajnas, penances and charities are synonymous with the word 'Sat'. The deed performed by an individual towards attaining salvation or Mokshya are no doubt 'Sat' or Satkarma so this word is very auspicious, divine and takes a person towards the Almighty or truth.

अश्रद्धया हुतं दत्तं तपस्तप्तं कृतं च यत् ।

असदित्युच्यते पार्थ न च तत्प्रेप्य नो इह ।। (XVII-28) ।।

O Arjun 'Faith' is very important and without 'faith' no work can be taken towards the logical conclusion. The Yajnas, charities and penances performed without faith do not result in any good or satisfaction. They as such are termed "Asatyajnas" and of no use.

Therefore, Yajnas, charities and penances must be performed with complete faith and dedication otherwise they do not result in any good. If the same are done with total faith and dedication the persons performing get happiness and salvation *i.e.*, Mokshya and are liberated from the cycle of births and deaths.

CHAPTER XVIII

The Lord is Explaining about Sanyas (asceticism) and Tyagas (renunciation). He is also Explaining in Details about Yajnas, Penances and Charities and Their Importance in the Life of an Individual

संन्यासस्य महाबाहो तत्त्वमिच्छामि वेदितुम् ।
यागस्य च हृषीकेश पृथक्केशिनिषूदन ।। (XVIII-1) ।।

Arjun asks O Hrishikesh (Krishna) I want to understand more about Sanyas (asceticism) and Tyaga (renunciation) separately. I request you to explain to me about both of them.

काम्यानां कर्मणां न्यासं सन्यासं कवयो विदुः ।
सर्वकर्मफलत्यागं प्राहुसत्यागं विचक्षणाः ।। (XVIII-2) ।।

O Arjun Tyags are of three types. The first is done on the daily basis *i.e.*, daily routine, doing worship, etc. This is termed Nitya (Tyag). The second type is done on special occasions *i.e.*, fasting or going to temple on a particular day this is termed as Naimittika. And the third type is which is done with a specific desire. This is termed as Kamya.

All the three are good for a person. The aim of all these is for the betterment of the mind.

त्याज्यं दोषवदित्येके कर्म प्राहुर्मनीषिणः ।
यज्ञदानतपः कर्म न त्याज्य मिति चापने ।। (XVIII-3) ।।

Some persons say that Yajnas, penances and charities should be discarded and there is no need of the same. But the majority feel that they are definitely helpful to the nature as well as to an individual as such they should be performed.

निश्चयं श्रृणु मे तत्र त्यागे भरत्स7त्तम ।
त्योगो ही पुरूषव्याध्र त्रिविधः सम्प्रकीर्तितः ।। (XVIII-4) ।।

O Bharata (Arjun) I would like to explain to you about the kind of renunciation (Tyag). They are of three kinds (*a*) Satva (*b*) Rajas (*c*) Tamas.

यज्ञदानतपः कर्म न त्याज्यं कार्यमेव तत् ।

यज्ञो दानं तपश्चैव पावनानि मनीषिणाम् ॥ (XVIII-5) ॥

Yajna, penance and charity should not be abandoned, actually they should be done as a duty because they purify both the body as well the soul.

एतान्यपि तु कर्माणि संगं त्यक्त्वा फलानि च ।

कर्तव्यानीति मे पार्थ निश्चितं मतमुत्तमम् ॥ (XVIII-6) ॥

O Parth (Arjun) these three acts are very pious and rewarding. Not only should we perform them regularly but other good acts as well to attain happiness, contentment and peace of mind. They are helpful to an individual for reaching to the ultimate truth *i.e.*, God.

नियतस्य तु संन्यासः कर्मणो नोपपद्यते ।

मोहात्तस्य परित्यागस्तामसः परिकीर्तितः ॥ (XVIII-7) ॥

The performing of your natural duties (*i.e.*, your duties towards parents, teacher, wife, children and society) should not be compromised at all. In fact that is the prime duty of an individual. What has been written in the religious books must be adhered to and practiced with will and faith, not-doing so is regarded as Tamasic.

दुःखमित्येव यत्कर्म कायक्लेश भ्यात्त्यजेत् ।

स कर्त्वा राजंस त्यागं नैव त्यागफल लभेत् ॥ (XVIII-8) ॥

Some persons feel that doing of Yajnas etc. is very difficult and do not perform the same due to the fear of difficulties, such a sacrifice is termed as Rajasic.

कार्यमित्येव यत्कर्म नियंत क्रियतेऽर्जुन ।

संगं त्यक्त्वा फलं चैव स त्यागः सत्त्विको मतः ॥ (XVIII-9) ॥

O Arjun he who believes in the religious books, does the duties with faith, not expecting any personal gains, such a sacrifice is Satva. A person who does the same, gains very much in life, as well as ensures the same after death also.

न द्वेष्टयकुशलं कर्म कुशले नानुषज्जते ।

त्यागी सत्वसमाविष्टो मेधावी छिन्नसंशयः ॥ 10 ॥

A true Yogi does not hate gainless Karmas and at the same time is detached from gainful Karmas. He comes in this world does all his duties towards the society in a positive state of mind. Helps everybody who comes in contact with him. After discharging his duties leaves this world quietly for the next journey.

न हि देहभृता शक्यं त्यक्तुं कर्माण्यशेषतः ।

यस्तु कर्मफलत्यागी स त्यागीत्यभिधीयते ॥ (XVIII-11) ॥

While living in this world, complete renunciation of all actions is not possible. But whatsoever we are able to achieve is helpful to a person. Those who do not expect anything in return are the real Karma Yogis.

अन्ष्टिमिष्टं मिश्रं च त्रिविधं कर्मणः फलम् ।

भवत्यत्यागिंना प्रेत्य न तु सन्यासिंना क्वचित् ॥ (XVIII-12) ॥

The actions (Karmas) done with a motive bear results good, average or bad, which a person carries to the next birth, they keep on accumulating. But to a Karma Yogi (ascetic) this does not apply, he does not have any credit or debit in his Karma account because he is above all these worldly desires and gets benefits beyond limits.

पंचैतानि महाबाहो कारणानि निबोध मे ।

सांख्ये कृतान्ते प्रोक्तानि सिद्धये सर्वकर्मणाम् ॥ (XVIII-13) ॥

O Arjun in Sankhya system of philosophy there are five factors which are mentioned for the successful accomplishment of all the Karmas (deeds). I will explain about the same to you.

अधिष्ठानं तथा कर्ता करणं च पृथग्विधम् ।

विविधाश्च पृथक्चेष्टा दैवं चैवात्र पंचमम् ॥ (XVIII-14) ॥

O Arjun the successful working of Karmas (deeds) depends on five factors.

(*i*) The seat of all actions *i.e.*, Body.

(*ii*) The individual working for it *i.e.* The doer.

(*iii*) The various kinds of instruments.

(*a*) Subjective (mind and senses)

(*b*) Objective (material objects).

(*iv*) The various operations involved in handling the instruments.

(*v*) The destiny of an individual. These five factors determine the success of the Karmas (deeds) of a person.

शरीरवांग्मनोभिर्यत्कर्म प्रारभते नरः ।

न्याय्यं वा विपरींत वा पंचैते तस्य हेतवः ।। (XVIII-15) ।।

These five factors are the cause of the Karmas (deeds) done through mind, speech and body by any individual.

तत्रैवं सति कर्तारमात्मानं केवलं तु यः ।

पश्चत्यकृतबुद्धित्वान्न स पश्यति दुर्मति ।। (XVIII-16) ।।

A person with negative tendencies or impure mind cannot understand this fact. He thinks that he himself is the doer of all the Karmas (deeds). He is unwise and fails to understand this truth.

यस्य नाहंकृतो भावो बुद्धिर्यस्य न लिप्यते ।

हत्वापि स इमांल्लोकान्न हन्ति न विबध्यते ।। (XVIII-17) ।।

A person whose conscious is clear and the mind unattached from the worldly attachments, he is blameless of any sin. The God forgives him for the sins he has committed.

But this should not be taken as a licence for doing sin or violence, it is said in a general way that God is very kind to a pious and spiritual person and forgives him of his all sins.

ज्ञानं ज्ञेयं परिज्ञाता त्रिविधा कर्मचोदना ।

करणं कर्म कर्तेति त्रिविधः कर्मसंग्रहः ।। (XVIII-18) ।।

The inspiration of all actions *i.e.*, Karmas or deeds are (*i*) knowledge (*ii*) The object of knowledge and (*iii*) knowledgeable. The combination of these inspire the desire to do Karma (deed) and a person is able to do any action. They all combine and give motivation to a person to do Karma as without doing the same no one can live in this world. This is the part of daily life and everyone does it.

ज्ञानं कर्म च कर्ता च त्रिधैव गुणभेदतः ।

प्रोच्यते गुणसंख्याने यथावच्छृणु तान्यपि ॥ (XVIII-19) ॥

Knowledge, Karma, and doer can be classified in three types *i.e.*, Satvic, Rajasic and Tamasic, where knowledge is Gyan, Karma is deed and doer is the individual who does the Karma (deed).

सर्वभूतेषु येनैकं भावमव्ययमीक्षते ।

अविभक्तं विभक्तेषु तज्ज्ञानं विद्धि सात्विकम् ॥ (XVIII-20) ॥

Satvic knowledge see's gods presence everywhere in all the creatures. The supreme power in all of them. This knowledge is positive is as such termed as Satvic.

पृथकत्वेन तु यज्ज्ञानं नाना भावा न्पृथग्विधान् ।

वेत्ति सर्वेषु भूतेषु तज्ज्ञानं विद्धि राजसम् ॥ (XVIII-21) ॥

When the knowledge sees difference in the species made by the Almighty *i.e.*, not understanding that the same soul is present in all the creations, this type of knowledge is known as Rajasic. He cannot acknowledge that all the living beings are similar and created by the same power supreme.

यत्तु कृत्स्नवदेकस्मिन्कार्ये सक्तमहैतुकम् ।

अतत्त्वार्थवदल्पं च तत्तामसमुदाहृतम् ॥ (XVIII-22) ॥

On the other hand a knowledge that feels that only body is everything and the soul is the part of the same body *i.e.*, destructible then the knowledge is termed as Tamasic. It does not see the difference between the soul and the body because whereas this body is temporary *i.e.*, destructible but the soul is eternal and never dies.

नियतं संगरहितमरागद्वेषतः कृतम् ।

अफलप्रेप्सुना कर्म यत्तत्सात्त्विकमुच्यते ॥ (XVIII-23) ॥

A Karma (deed) done with religious state of mind and with positive intentions is termed as Satvic Karma.

यत्तु कामेप्सुना कर्म साहंकारेण वा पुनः ।

क्रियते बहुलायासं तद्राजसमुदाहृतम् ॥ (XVIII-24) ॥

A Karma (deed) performed with ego or boastful intentions and just for a show is Rajasic Karma. It is not done with pious bent of mind or intentions. This type of Karma is not fruitful.

अनुबन्धं क्षयं हिंसामनवेक्ष्य च पौरूषम् ।

मोहादारभ्यते कर्म यत्ततामसमुच्यते ॥ (XVIII-25) ॥

Similarly a Karma done without thinking of its results or by harming somebody or with violence is of no use and it is termed as Tamasic Karma.

मुक्तसंगोऽनहंवादी धृत्युत्साहसमन्वितः ।

सिद्धयसिद्धयोर्निर्विकारः कर्ता सात्विक उच्यते ॥ (XVIII-26) ॥

A person who is not boastful, pious, happy, remains always positive in his approach, remains calm in success or failure is a Satvic doer.

रागी कर्मफलप्रेप्सुर्लुब्धो हिंसात्मकोऽशुचिः ।

हर्षशोकान्वितः कर्ता राजसः परिकीर्तितः ॥ 27 ॥

A person who is greedy, always think of the results in his favour, effected by joys and sorrows in life is a Rajasic doer.

अयुक्तः प्राकृतः स्तब्धः शठो नैष्कृतिकोऽलसः ।

विषादी दीर्घसूत्री च कर्ता तामस उच्यते ॥ (XVIII-28) ॥

A person who is deceitful, is harmful to others, jealous, lazi, arrogant, this is the example of a Tamasic doer.

बुद्धेर्भेदं घृतेश्चैव गुणतस्त्रिविधं श्रृणु ।
प्रोच्यमानमशेषेण पृथक्त्वेन धनंजय ।। (XVIII-29) ।।

O Dhananjaya (Arjun) I will now tell you about the three types of Wisdoms (minds).

प्रवृतिं च निवृत्तिं च कार्याकार्ये भयाभये ।
बन्धंमोक्षं च या वेत्ति बुद्धिः सा पार्थ सात्त्विकी ।। (XVIII-30) ।।

O Parth (Arjun), the wisdom that generates pious and positive thoughts in others, inspires freedom, fearlessness, shows right path to others, spreads spiritualism is termed as Satvic wisdom (Mind).

यया धर्ममधर्म च कार्य चाकार्यमेव च ।
अयथावत्प्रजानाति बुद्धिः सा पार्थ राजसी ।। (XVIII-31) ।।

O Parth (Arjun), the wisdom (Mind) that spreads wrong thoughts and cannot correct the wrong causes, cannot undo the wrong knowingly is Rajasic wisdom.

अर्धम धर्ममिति या मन्यते तमसावृता ।
सर्वार्थान्विपरीतांश्च बुद्धिः सा पार्थ तामसी ।। (XVIII-32) ।।

O Parth, Tamasic wisdom spreads evil and gives wrong notions about religion and always give negative signals to society. This wisdom is never helpful to the mankind and always gives harm.

धृत्या यया धारयते मनः प्राणेन्द्रियक्रियाः ।
योगेनाव्यभिचारिण्या धृतिः सा पार्थ सात्त्विकी ।। (XVIII-33) ।।

O Parth forbearance (patience) self control is also of three types *i.e.*, Satvic, Rajasic and Tamasic. The control over mind, heart and senses is a Satvic forbearance. It requires a lot of practice and hard work to have control over them as such it is Satvic forbearance.

यया तु धर्मकामार्थान्धृत्या धारयतेऽजुर्न ।
प्रसंगेन फलाकांक्षी धृतिः सा पार्थ राजसी ।। (XVIII-34) ।।

The forbearance shown in doing the work of dharma, gaining wealth with hard work, to have desire to have more is termed as Rajasic.

यया स्वप्नं भयं शोकं विषादं मदमेव च ।

न विमुंचति दुर्मेधा धृतिः सा पार्थ तामसी ॥ (XVIII-35) ॥

O Parth, forbearance (patience) which gives an evil person to bear fear, worry and pain etc. is termed as Tamasic. An evil person spreads evil, he has to bear patience to accept fear, worry and pain in return. So the negative type of forbearance is Tamasic in nature.

सुखं त्विदानीं त्रिविधं श्रृणु मे भरतर्षभ ।

अभ्यासाद्रमते यत्र दुःखान्त च निगच्छति ॥ (XVIII-36) ॥

O Bharta (Arjun) now I will explain to you regarding the types of happiness. They are also of three types *i.e.*, Satvic, Rajastic and Tamasic.

The happiness a person gets by doing pious and spiritual deeds, the one he gets by serving his Guru (teacher), parents, wife and children, by serving the mankind in general, by doing positive deeds, by helping people in distress is Satvic happiness.

यत्तदग्रे विषमिव परिणामेऽमृतोपमम ॥

तत्सुखं सात्विकं प्रोक्तमात्मबुद्धिप्रसादजम् ॥ (XVIII-37) ॥

In the initial stages the happiness might not be there, but the final end is of great satisfication and fulfilment and full of happiness. That is why it is termed as Satvic happiness.

विषयेन्द्रिय संयोगाद्यतदग्रेऽमृतोपमम ।

परिणामे विषमिव तत्सुखं राजंस स्मृतम ॥ (XVIII-38) ॥

The attitude of eat, drink and be merry gives a lot of pleasure and happiness to a person, but the end result is unhappiness of this attitude. This is Rajasic happiness.

यदग्रे चानुबन्धे च सुखं मोहनमात्मनः ।

निद्रालस्य प्रमादोत्थं तत्तामसमुदाहृतम् ॥ (XVIII-39) ॥

The happiness gained by any person by harming the others, the exhibition of wealth, lavish spending, laziness, to much sleeping are termed as Tamasic happiness.

न तदस्ति पृथिव्यां वा दिवि देवेषु वा पुनः ।
सत्वं प्रकृतिजैर्मुक्तं यदेभिः स्यातित्रभिर्गुणै ।। (XVIII-40) ।।

O Arjun no one is in this world who does not have any of these traits. They are universal and can be seen everywhere throughout the world.

ब्राह्मणक्षत्रियविंशा शूद्राणं च परंतप ।
कर्माणि प्रविभक्तानि स्वभावप्रभवैर्गुणैः ।। (XVIII-41) ।।

O Arjun all the four castes *i.e.*, Brahman, Kshatriya, Vaishya and Shudra have been assigned the duties according to the traits & capibilities in them. Krishna is summing up and telling Arjun about the same, what he had told him earlier as well.

शमो हमस्तपः शौचं क्षान्तिरार्जवमेव च ।
ज्ञानं विज्ञानमास्तिक्यं ब्रह्मकर्म स्वभावजम् ।। (XVIII-42) ।।

The duties of the Brahman is to preach and interpret Vedas and the other spiritual books and give education to all others, teaching about purity of thoughts, senses control and integrity, etc.

शौर्य तेजो धृतिर्दाक्ष्यं युद्धे चाप्यपलायनम् ।
दानमीश्वरभावश्च क्षात्रं कर्म स्वभावजम् ।। (XVIII-43) ।।

The duties of the Kshatriya are defending the country from external as well as the internal enemies. Defending the weak from the stronger with their bravery, defeat the enemies and secure the country, do charity, etc.

कृषिगौरक्ष्य वाणिज्य वैश्यकर्म स्वभावजम् ।
परिचर्यात्मक कर्म शुद्रस्यापि स्वभावजम् ।। (XVIII-44) ।।

The duties of Vaishya are to do commerce, agriculture, cattle rearing, looking after the industry, producing enough of foodgrains so that no one goes hungry in the country.

While the duties of Shudra are to serve the rest.

स्वे स्वे कर्मण्यभिरतः संसिद्धिलभते नरः ।
स्वकर्मनिरतः सिद्धिं यथा विन्दति तच्छृणु ॥ (XVIII-45) ॥

Every person doing his duty in a systemic manner so that all are happy and contented. All are helping one another and contributing their best for the country. All are performing their duties honestly and keeping Almighty in hearts, so that there is happiness all around.

यतः प्रवृतिर्भूतानां येन सर्वमिंद ततम् ।
स्वकर्मणा तमभ्यर्च्य सिद्धिं विन्दति मानवः ॥ (XVIII-46) ॥

A person gets perfection and peace of mind by remembering God and discharging his duties honestly. By worship and meditation he always remains positive in his approach and does his duties in a calm and composed state of mind. When everything is done in accordance with the will of God there will be happiness and positive developments everywhere.

श्रेयान्स्वधर्मो विगुणः परधर्मात्स्वनुष्ठितात् ।
स्वभावनियंत कर्म कुर्वन्नाप्नोति किल्विषम् ॥ (XVIII-47) ॥

Your own faith is supreme and gives happiness and satisfaction. So a person should keep himself in his own faith and should not adopt any other.

सहजं कर्म कौन्तेय सदोषमपि न त्यजेत् ।
सर्वारम्भा हि दोषेण धूमेनाग्निरिवावृता ॥ (XVIII-48) ॥

O son of Kunti (Arjun) at no cost one should discard his own faith for another. Because no faith is complete or perfect in itself, all have some short comings. Therefore, one must adhere to his own faith at all costs.

असक्तबुद्धि सर्वत्र जितात्मा विगतस्पृहः ।
नैष्कर्म्यसिद्धिं परमां संन्यासेनाधिगच्छति ॥ (XVIII-49) ॥

But a perfect person always reaches the God in whatever faith he follows. Therefore, one should not change his faith for reaching the almighty. Only there should be a strong faith to attain Him. All faiths lead to the same goal. There are many ways to reach God, but at the same time complete positive approach, faith, determination and patience are required. As such a person should stick to his own faith at all costs.

सिद्धिं प्राप्तोयथा ब्रह्म तथाप्नोति निबोध में ।
समासेनैव कौन्तेय निष्ठा ज्ञानस्य या परा ।। (XVIII-50) ।।

O son of Kunti (Arjun) many persons have attained God through Sankhya Yoga (Gyan or love) and there are many others who have attained him through Wisdom Yoga. I will tell you about attributes and signs of such persons.

बुद्धया विशुद्धया युक्तो धृत्यात्मानं नियम्य च ।
शब्दादीन्विषयांस्त्कत्वा रागद्वेषौ व्युदस्य च ।। (XVIII-51) ।।

A person who attains pure wisdom through Sankhya Yoga, he has full control on desires. He feels no difference between love and hatred, free from lust, anger, greed, attachment, ego and jealousy. He loves God and society and is always helpful to needy and downtrodden.

विविक्तसेवी लघ्वाशी यतवाक्कायमानसः ।
ध्यानयोगपरो नित्यं वैराग्यं समुपाश्रितः ।। (XVIII-52) ।।

He loves solitude and does meditation regularly. He has full control over mind, body, speech and conscious. Full of confidence and away from all the negative tendencies.

अहंकार बलदर्प काम क्रोध परिग्रहम ।
विमुच्य निर्ममः शान्तो ब्रह्मभूयाय कल्पते ।। (XVIII-53) ।।

He is a person who does not have pride does not show off his strength, away from the negative tendencies. He is of peaceful nature but not coward. He is fearless and strong believer in truth. Respectful to all and devoid of any ill will towards anyone.

ब्रह्मभूतः प्रसन्मात्मा न शोचति न कांक्षति ।
समः सर्वेषु भूतेषु मभ्दक्तिं लभेत पराम् ।। (XVIII-54) ।।

He is always cheerful, does not feel helpless in any situation, faces the adversities with determination and strength, is fearless, does not expect anything from anyone. Such a happy soul is sure to reach salvation or Mokshya.

भक्त्या मामभिजानाति यावान्यश्चास्मि तत्त्वतः ।
तत्तो मां तत्त्वतो ज्ञात्वा विशते तदनन्तरम् ।। (XVIII-55) ।।

With faith in Me (God) he leaves everything at My discretion because he knows that I am the supreme authority and all is my creation on this earth. With this confidence he reaches Me and gets complete salvation or Mokshya.

सर्वकर्माण्यपि सदा कुर्वाणो मद्व्यपाश्रयः ।
मत्प्रसादादवाप्नोति शाश्वतं पदमव्ययम् ।। (XVIII-56) ।।

Such a devotee attains complete peace of mind and salvation and gets the blessing of God. He free's himself from all the bindings and does not come back in this world again to undergo sufferings.

चेतसा सर्वकर्मणि मयि संन्यस्य मत्परः ।
बुद्धियोगमुपाश्रित्य मच्चित्तः सततं भव ।। (XVIII-57) ।।

O Arjun submit all your Karmas (deeds) at the altar of God, come under his protection. Your thoughts should be in search of almighty. With these pious actions there is no doubt that you will attain complete salvation and peace not only in this world but in the next birth as well. You should have pure and pious desire to reach God. He never lets down his devotees.

मच्चितः सर्वदुर्गाणि मत्प्रसादात्तरिष्यसि ।
अथ चेत्त्वमंहकारान्न श्रोष्यसि विंनक्ष्यसि ।। (XVIII-58) ।।

O Arjun therefore submit with total dedication to the supreme power (God). Offer all your karmas (deeds) to Him. The God will take you under his protection and with his blessings you will be able to come out of all your difficulties in life. But due to ego if you do not submit then only sufferings and failures will encircle you.

This will give you only worry, anxiety and repentance. Therefore, O Arjun submit to the Almighty and leave all your problems to Him. He will definitely come to your help.

In the name of Arjun Lord Krishna in other words is addressing the mankind in general, what he said to Arjun is applicable to all the mankind, to be God fearing, do good and pious deeds in life. Do not be boastful and challenge the authority of God, because that will only harm the individual. So it is in our own interest to do positive deeds in our lives so that at the time of departure (death) we should go gracefully and peacefully without any repentance.

यदहंकारमाश्रित्य न योत्स्य इति मन्यसे ।

मिथ्यैष व्यवसायस्ते प्रकृतिस्त्वां नियोक्ष्यति ।। (XVIII-59) ।।

O Arjun inspite of all this if you try to stay away from this war due to your ego, that will not do any justice either to you or your family. Your mind will also not agree to this and will force you to do the duty. The warrior in you will also not allow you to runaway and not to fight this holy war.

At this stage Krishna was convinced that he was able to remove the doubts in Arjun's mind regarding the war with Kauravas. That is why he is telling him that his warrior instinct will not allow Arjun to go back and not to fight, because his conscious will not permit him. Krishna was happy and convinced that he was able to remove the doubts in his mind regarding the war.

स्वभावजेन कौन्तेय निबद्धः स्वेन कर्मणां ।

कर्तुं नेच्छसि यन्मोहात्करिष्यस्यवशोऽपि तत् ।। (XVIII-60) ।।

O son of Kunti (Arjun) the duty what you are supposed to do, but unable to do due to attachments is not right. Inspite of that your conscious will not allow you to react otherwise. The soldier or warrior in you will drive for the war. Therefore, you should not bind yourself inspite of the fact that the opponents standing in front of you are your own kith and kins.

ईश्वरः सर्वभूतानां हृद्देशेऽर्जुन तिष्ठति ।
भ्रामयन्सर्वभूतानि यन्त्रारूढानि मायया ॥ (XVIII-61) ॥

O Arjun God is omnipresent in the universe. He lives in the hearts of all the living beings, and blesses by his divine power according to the Karmas done. In other words the almighty awards everyone according to the good or bad karmas done by him on this earth.

All individuals reap the harvest of their own good or bad Karmas. Good leads to peace and Mokshya while bad leads to unhappiness and sufferings.

तमेव शरणं गच्छ सर्वभावेन भारत ।
तत्प्रसादात्परां शान्तिं स्थानं प्राप्स्यसि शाश्वतम् ॥ (XVIII-62) ॥

Therefore O Arjun go under the protection of the power supreme (God). His bleassings will give you total salvation, peace of mind and you will come out from the cycle of births and deaths and attain Mokshya.

Once a person understands that God is the ultimate force who is the creator and destroyer of this universe, he gets peace of mind. A wise and pious devotee leaves everything in his hands. The duty of a person is to do karma with pure and determined mind and leave the rest to God. Now it becomes the duty of the Almighty to award accordingly.

When we do this, peace and a sense of fulfillment comes to a person and he is ready to receive what comes out of the same. The mind and heart come in the state of complete peace, worries and anxieties disappear.

इति ते ज्ञानमाख्यातं गुह्याद्गुह्यतरं मया ।
विमृश्यैतदशेषेण यथेच्छसि तथा कुरू ॥ (XVIII-63) ॥

O Arjun I have revealed to you the deepest of the secrets of life and soul. Now you are the best judge to checkout your own path in life as per your wisdom.

Krishna does not force anything on Arjun. He leaves it to him to make up his mind. He says to Arjun that he has explained all what was expected of him. So he leaves the rest to him to be decided whether to fight or not. In other words, he is not forcing Arjun for the final decision, he leaves everything at his discretion whether to fight or surrender.

As the parents bring up the child, give him protection, education, guidance and when he grows up leave him to decide for his career and other problems of life himself so that he gains confidence to face the world. In the same way the Lord tells Arjun that he has explained all what he knew and now the rest is left to him to decide, the course of action he feels is best for himself and his army.

सर्वगुह्यतमं भूयःश्रृणु में परमं वचः ।
इष्टोऽसि मे दृढमिति ततो वक्ष्यामि ते हितम् ।। (XVIII-64) ।।

As there was no immediate reaction from Arjun, Krishna says again "O Arjun I will tell you more secret of the secrets once again, because you have come to me for guidance. Therefore, I explain to you which will give a lot of more information for your knowledge and help you a lot indeed. I am doing this all because you are my disciple and I have a great love for you.

In the name of Arjun the Lord is giving a message to the mankind.

मन्मना भव मभ्द्क्तो मद्याजी मां नमस्कुरु ।
मामेवैष्यसि सत्यं ते प्रतिजाने प्रियोऽसि मे ।। (XVIII-65) ।।

O Arjun concentrate your mind and thoughts towards God, bow to him with deep love and affection. He will definitely come to your help and show you the right path.

If a devotee prays to the Almighty with pure and pious mind the God definitely listens and come to his rescue, this I can assure you (Arjun).

सर्वधर्मान्परित्यज्य मामेकं शरणं व्रज ।
अहं त्वा सर्वपापेभ्यो मोक्षयिष्यामि मा शुचः ।। (XVIII-66) ।।

So Arjun leave aside all your inhibitions and come to the door of the power supreme (God). He will definitely help you and free you from all worries, wrongs and sins. Do not at all worry at all as the God is always near you.

Here the Lord ensures the devotees at large. He says the person who remembers God with pious intentions and pure conscious, the God will definitely come and stand by the devotee in time of need. This is the assurance being given by the Lord to Arjun and the humanity at large. There should be strength and purity in the devotee and the God will not disappoint him or leave him in difficulty in the time of need.

इदं ते नातपस्काय नाभक्ताय कदाचन ।
न चाशुश्रूषवे वाच्यं न च मां योऽभ्यसूयति ॥ (XVIII-67) ॥

O Arjun I have disclosed this knowledge (Gita) to you because you are my devotee and have full faith in the Almighty. This knowledge should not be given to a non-believer, have doubts regarding the power supreme and do not have an urge to meet him. This knowledge be given to those who are keen to have it.

य इमं परमं गुह्यं मभ्द्क्तेष्वभिधास्यति ।
भक्ति मयि परां कृत्वा मामेवैष्यत्यसंशयः ॥ (XVIII-68) ॥

O Arjun a devotee who has love and respect for the God and gives this knowledge (about Gita) to others who are keen to receive it, he too will get the divine blessings. There should not be any doubt regarding this. The Lord says that the spreading of this message is equally pious and rewarding. He too will get the divine blessings and reaches the Almighty at the end of his life in this world.

न च तस्मान्ममुष्येषु कशिचन्मे प्रियकृत्तमः ।
भविता न च मे तस्मादन्यः प्रियतरो भुवि ॥ (XVIII-69) ॥

A person who is spreading this knowledge is very dear to me. He will be near me at all the time and God will help him in every possible way. In the other words the lord is assuring that the reading and listening and giving the knowledge of Gita is equally pious and helpful to a devotee. With its help he can discover happiness and complete salvation or Mokshya.

अध्येष्यते च य इमं धर्म्यं संवादमावयोः ।
ज्ञानयज्ञेन तेनाहमिष्टः सयामिति मे मतिः ॥ (XVIII-70) ॥

O Arjun the reading of Gita is equal to the worship of God. The person who will tell about this dialogue between you and me and explains to others will be blessed by the Almighty and will attain salvation or Mokshya. He will come out of the cycle of births and deaths.

श्रद्धावाननसूयश्च श्रणुयादपि यो नरः ।
सोऽपि मुक्तः शुभांल्लोकान्प्राप्नुयातं पुण्यकर्मणाम् ।। (XVIII-71) ।।

O Arjun who reads Gita will be benefitted in life, even listening of the same will give enormous gains to the devotee. The individuals who do so will free themselves from the continuous process of life and death. They will attain total peace of mind and after death go to the abode of God *i.e.*, heaven. They need not come back on this earth to undergo the cycle of birth and death. They will receive Mokshya or complete bliss from the power supreme (God).

कच्चिदेतच्छतं पार्थ त्वयैकाग्रेण चेतसा ।
कच्चिदज्ञानसम्मोहः प्रनष्टस्ते धनंजय ।। (XVIII-72) ।।

O Parth (Arjun) tell me if your doubts are clear now? or still you feel confused in your mind about the soul and the body? Please let me know if you still hold any doubts or confusion about life and soul?

At this point Krishna was confident that he was able to remove the doubts and confusions from Arjun's mind. But still he wanted to confirm the same from Arjun. Therefore he asks him to confirm about the same.

नष्टो मोहः स्मृतिर्लब्धा त्वत्प्रसादान्मयाच्युत ।
स्थितोऽस्मि गतसन्देहः। करिष्यं वचनं तव ।। (XVIII-73) ।।

Arjun replies O Krishna all my doubts and confusions have disappeared and I am completely free of them. My attachments have also been destroyed, I can think and see things clearly with a determined and resolute mind. I will definitely do and act as per your direction and fight.

Here the Lord has given the message to the mankind, never to be disheartened in life. Remove all doubts and confusions from mind and keep the struggle on, without giving up till the victory is achieved.

इत्यहं वायुदेवस्य पार्थस्य च महात्मनः ।
संवादमिममश्रौषमभ्दुंत रोमहर्षणम् ।। (XVIII-74) ।।

Sanjay has been explaining regarding the events of the war to king Dhritrashta. He says O king I have heard the conversation between Lord Krishna and warrior Arjun in the battle field of Kurukshetra and have communicated the same to you in detail.

व्यासप्रसादाच्छ्रुतवाने तद्गुह्यमहं परम् ।
योगं योगेश्वरात्कृष्णात्साक्षात्कथयतः स्वयंम् ।। (XVIII-75) ।।

O king I could see and hear about this secret conversation between Lord Krishna and Arjun taking place at the battle field of Kurukshetra due to the blessings of sage Vedvyasa. He had bestowed this power to me so that I could tell you all about the same.

राजन्सस्मृत्य संस्मृत्य संवाद मिममभ्दुतम् ।
केशवार्जुनयोः पुण्यहृष्यामि च मुहुमुर्हुः ।। (XVIII-76) ।।

Sanjay says O king at this time I think about this divine and mysterious conversation between Krishna and Arjun. I feel extremely joyous because it was so divine and full of knowledge.

तच्च संस्मृत्य संस्मृत्य रूपमत्यभ्दुतं हरेः ।
विस्मयो मे महान् राजन्हृष्यामि च पुनः पुनः ।। (XVIII-77) ।।

O king I visualize again and again of the divine spectacle shown by Lord Krishna to Arjun about his divine, awesome and mysterious form. The more I think about it the more joyous I feel. It was so wonderful and awesome that the same does not go away from my memory. There is overwhelming sense of joy in me.

यत्र योगेश्वरः कृष्णो यत्र पार्थो धनुर्धरः ।
तत्र श्रोर्विजयो भूतिर्धुवा नीतिर्मतिर्मम ।। (XVIII-78) ।।

O king on which side Lord Krishna and warrior Arjun are, the victory will also be on that side. I do not have any doubts about the outcome of this war. This is my conviction that Krishna and Arjun are going to win this war.

OM-TAT-SAT

EPILOGUE

Bhagwat Gita is like a vast and deep ocean. I tried to take few drops out of it. How far I could achieve the same, I leave this to the judgement of my esteem readers. As far as I am concerned it was a unique spiritual journey and divine bliss.

As the time passes many more like me will also be inspired to take a few drops from this vast ocean (Bhagwat Git) share with others as per their understanding. For me it was really a sublime experience. It took me about an year to complete this work and I am extremely happy to share the same with you.

R.K.N. Bali

22.2.08

New Delhi